Published by
The Fruitmarket Gallery Edinburgh
Locus+ Publishing Ltd Newcastle upon Tyne

ISBN 1 899377 21 2

NATHAN COLEY

There will be no miracles here

Contents /

6_____Texts /

Texts /

Building the Imagination
Fiona Bradley

*In vain, great-hearted Kublai, shall I attempt
to describe Zaira, city of high bastions. I
could tell you how many steps make up the
streets rising like stairways, and the degree
of the arcades' curves, and what kind of zinc
scales cover the roofs; but I already know
this would be the same as telling you
nothing. The city does not consist of this, but
of the relationships between the
measurements of its space and the events of
its past; the height of a lamppost and the
distance from the ground of a hanged
usurper's swaying feet; the line strung from
the lamppost to the railing opposite and the
festoons that decorate the course of the
queen's nuptial procession; the height of that
railing and the leap of the adulterer who
climbed over it at dawn; the tilt of a guttering
and a cat's progress along it as he slips into
the same window; the firing range of a
gunboat which has suddenly appeared
beyond the cape and the bomb that
destroys the guttering; the rips in the fish net
and the three old men seated on the dock
mending nets and telling each other for the
hundredth time the story of the gunboat of
the usurper, who some say was the queen's
illegitimate son, abandoned in his swaddling
clothes there on the dock.*

ITALO CALVINO, *INVISIBLE CITIES*, 1972

Italo Calvino's *Invisible Cities* conjures cities
in the imagination, describing some in terms
of memory or desire; others as thin cities,
trading cities, continuous cities, hidden cities;
still others as cities in the sky or cities of the
dead. Famously, the imaginary cities, with
their extravagantly feminine names – Dionira,
Isidora, Penthesilia – are all one city: Venice.
    Calvino's insistence, throughout his
descriptions of Venice, on the gap between
the city as built and as experienced, as it
exists in the world and in the mind and
memory, resonates throughout Nathan
Coley's practice. Working predominantly with
urban spaces, Coley also conjures cities,
metaphorically dismantling them in order to
understand why and how they came to exist,
then rebuilding them as places to be re-
imagined according to individual knowledge
and experience. Sometimes the artist works
with whole cities, sometimes individual
buildings, fragments of buildings or sites for
buildings. Some of the places on which he
fixes his gaze exist in the world, some only in
the past or in some conjectured future.
Some occupy fixed points, and some are
mobile between points. Common to them all
is the idea that we get the cities we imagine
and that they in turn shape for us the future
we deserve. As in Calvino's Zaira, Coley's
urban spaces have meaning because of their
past, but they store this meaning as lessons
for the future, if only their inhabitants can
learn to read the signs:

*The city [...] does not tell its past, but
contains it like the lines of a hand, written in
the corners of the streets, the gratings of the
windows, the banisters of the steps, the
antennae of the lightning rods, the poles of
the flags, every segment marked in turn with
scratches, indentations, scrolls.*

    The artist's work begins as a critique of
urbanism, often focusing on the difference
between the deliberate and the unintentional
in urban space – the kind of 'accidental
architecture' that happens round the edges
of urban planning, the things that happen to
space as people live in it. *Pigeon Lofts*,
1997 (pp.40–43), is one of the earliest – and
funniest – works to address this. Set up as a
slide lecture and purporting to be a dry

discourse on the finer points of an architect's practice, *Pigeon Lofts* takes the viewer on a magical mystery tour of Glasgow's back yards, looking at the bizarre, yet bizarrely standardised structures that people build to house their pigeons. Over the changing images comes a woman's voice extolling the virtues of each minute variation in design – 'this is one of our most popular models ...'.

Fourteen Churches of Münster, 2000 (pp.62–65), marks a shift in the work, and a move towards the examination of urban architecture, whether accidental or otherwise, as a social and political signifier – an index of experience and a marker for life lived. The work is an aerial video of the city of Münster, the flight path determined by the location of the churches that ring the city. Using churches as navigational aids acknowledges their importance in a predominantly Catholic city, but it also makes chilling reference to the callous and casual use made of religious buildings in Second World War bombing raids. Pilots were instructed to aim for a city's cathedral – the very building which marks it out as a city – and drop their bombs on that.

Pigeon Lofts and *Fourteen Churches of Münster*, though firmly rooted in the real in the mechanics of their presentation in a gallery – one a slide lecture with attendant trappings of chairs, projector and screen, the other a single screen video on a television monitor – are, at the point of their engagement with the built environment they reference, ephemeral. *Homes for Heroes*, 2001 (pp.72–73), with its similarly understated yet resonant wartime reference is an altogether more solid proposition. As sculpture, it brings an element of the real environment tangibly into the gallery, replicating in miniature a particular,

dilapidated building, and pulling together the facts of its past and the uncertain potential for it to have a future. In conversation the artist characterises this work, and ~~Hurt~~ *Burn me Daddy*, the companion piece with which it is regularly shown, as objects which 'don't really know what they are. They are not sure if they are models of distressed buildings or distressed models of buildings'. Like cities, they need to be experienced, lived in, looked at and used before they, and we, can know.

Uncertainty has little place in *The Land Marked*, 2001 (pp.76–81), which uses the rhetoric of large-scale projection to look at the way a city's past has an inescapable effect on its present and future. In Belém, part of the city of Lisbon, the land is marked – literally – by a fifteenth-century tower which stands on the edge of the city, looking out to sea. Contested, neglected and much-restored throughout its history, the tower is now a source of national pride and is protected by legislation from any physical or conceptual encroachment. Coley, making an exhibition for the new Centro Cultural de Belém, a vast white contemporary building whose construction so close to the tower caused outrage in the city, chose to blow the tower up. In an animation rather than in actuality, but his action, in a neat confirmation of the importance of the imaginary where cities are concerned, still made the national news.

In making *The Land Marked*, Coley acted as an individual threatening public property, and many of his ideas work the territory between the private and the public. He has quite literally occupied public space, making works of public sculpture such as *The Italian Tower*, 2001 (pp.82–83) and *Show Home*, 2003 (pp.92–97), elaborate fictions involving the construction and temporary erection of a putative Italianate tower on the one hand and a facsimile of a newly-developed private house on the other. Whether making so-called public works of art or those intended for exhibition indoors in a gallery context, he often works on the margin between the private and the public – the space, for example, in which an individual's private property may become evidence to be held up in a public trial. This was part of what interested the artist during his time as an unofficial court artist at the trial in 2000 of the two Libyans accused of bombing Pan Am flight 103 over Lockerbie in 1988. Much of the work that resulted from his attendance at the trial, *Lockerbie*, 2003 (pp.98–105) maps the process by which the private becomes public and the insignificant significant. Evidence was presented to the court in the form of photographs – of the briefcase in which the bomb was supposed to have been planted, of fragments of that briefcase, of a label from a pair of trousers, of the receipt for the purchase of those trousers. The artist made twelve drawings of these photographs, laborious transcriptions reminiscent of the work of a court artist.

The activity of transcription, and the labour it entails, is a constant within Coley's practice. Just as, in multiply describing it, Calvino somehow stakes a claim to Venice, Coley's insistent unmaking and remaking of elements of the built environment makes them peculiarly his own. Whether he is photographing, filming, animating, drawing or making models, Coley's approach to the spaces and buildings on which he focuses is remarkably hands-on for an artist whose work has its roots in urbanism and social and architectural theory. Nowhere is this more evident than in the two works *The Lamp of Sacrifice, 161 Places of Worship,*

Birmingham 2000 (pp.68–71) and *The Lamp of Sacrifice, 286 Places of Worship, Edinburgh 2004* (pp.110–117) which confirm the artist's commitment to architecture as an agent of social and political change. Both these works involve the artist capturing an entire city by making models of every single place of worship listed in the relevant Yellow Pages. From Catholic church to mosque, Presbyterian hall to Quaker meeting house, the models between them summon the entire city and the shifting communities and neighbourhoods of which it consists.

In these works, Coley consummately describes the cities he addresses, and in terms of which Calvino's narrator might approve. By rebuilding them from one particular perspective, he brings experience as well as scrutiny to bear. This is his method: to describe by remaking so that he, and by extension the viewer, has a physical as well as mental relationship to the space in question. Cities, and the buildings that bring them into being, are physical things – we walk through them, know them first with our feet and understand them best through the time they take from us. Working to turn information into knowledge, Coley's interrogation of the seen and unseen systems by which our built environment is structured is a time-consuming and intensely active process. Even when taking the decision to make a public sculpture in the form of a book – as with **Urban Sanctuary**, 1997 (pp.26–35) – the artist still insists on the experiential quality of the work. 'I am building an urban sanctuary', he announces at the start of one of the interviews that were always intended to take the place of the actual body of the supposed sanctuary. But build a sanctuary, of course, is exactly what the book does.

Politics of Space

Architecture, Truth, and other Fictions in the work of Nathan Coley
Susanne Gaensheimer

In the summer of 2000, Nathan Coley travelled from Dundee, a post-industrial harbour city on the east coast of Scotland where the artist has lived and worked for several years, to the very small and normally quite unremarkable village of Zeist in the heart of the Netherlands. He took a train from Dundee to Edinburgh, flew from Edinburgh to Amsterdam, boarded another train to Utrecht, and then waited for a bus to Zeist. Having arrived there, he set out on foot to Kamp van Zeist, a former US Army base. Although Coley had already been travelling through Holland for a whole day to get to his remote destination, the policeman who greeted him at the entrance to Kamp van Zeist was not Dutch, but Scottish. The moment he set foot in the former military base, Coley was in Scottish territory. The Lockerbie trial had been in progress there since April 2000.

On 22 December 1988, an aircraft of the American airline Pan Am was blown up over Lockerbie, a small town in Scotland. The 259 passengers and crew on the flight and 11 residents of Lockerbie were killed in the disaster. The bomb was disguised as a radio recorder and had been smuggled on to the flight in a briefcase at Malta Airport. The plane was scheduled to fly from Malta to Frankfurt, then to London, and finally to New York. Had the bomb detonated only a few minutes earlier or later, the plane would not have crashed in Lockerbie. However, the timing of the blast made Lockerbie the scene of a terrorist act which was not aimed at Scotland at all, but at the United States. After 13 years of intensive investigations, suspicion fell on two Libyans who had been employed as ground crew at Malta Airport at the time of the attack. On the basis of the evidence, the suspects were charged with mass murder under Scottish law. After a 14-month trial

based on circumstantial evidence, one of the two suspects (Al Megrahi) was found guilty and sentenced to 25 years' imprisonment in a Scottish jail, while the other was acquitted. Because of the politically sensitive nature of this issue, the trial was held on 'neutral' ground in the Netherlands, where a Scottish court of law was set up within the guarded perimeter of Kamp van Zeist. Thus a part of Scotland found itself situated in mainland Europe for the duration of the trial – a strategy known to lawyers as a 'legal fiction'.

This abstract definition of a country's territory on the basis of a legal declaration, which has nothing to do with the historical development of a specific place or with actual sensory perception, is symptomatic of the way people in the modern world have become fundamentally estranged from their surroundings. Hannah Arendt, in *Vita Activa* (Piper, Munich 1960), argues that this increasing estrangement from the world began at a very early date, on the threshold of the modern age. She links this phenomenon to certain events which, significantly, had something to do with traumatic changes to people's sense of space. These events were the discovery of America and then Europe's efforts to colonise other continents; the Reformation, which led to confiscations of land belonging to the church and monasteries and which set in motion the processes of accumulation characteristic of modern economics; and, finally, the invention of the telescope and the development of new measuring technologies which defined the earth as an abstract sphere and reduced to measurable dimensions those real distances which, until then, it had been impossible to calculate or bridge except by expending significant proportions of a human lifetime. As remote as these events may seem in history, it is nonetheless clear that the new relationship of human beings to space which they imply is the origin of those processes of estrangement which define us today, in the postmodern age of globalisation. For example, the rapid pace of developments in transport and communications technologies since the 19th century has made it easier and easier to cross vast distances and ultimately has led to the creation of a global network which affects all aspects of life. National borders and physical distances between countries and continents are increasingly perceived as abstract quantities. The worldwide processes of liberalisation and democratisation after the Second World War and after the end of the Cold War have eroded the political and strategic definitions of national borders. However, while these processes brought about an increase in people's freedom of movement, they also meant that people were uprooted as traditional cultural communities dissolved, and a global stream of refugees and migrants was set in motion.

Transferring the Scottish law court to Kamp van Zeist in the Netherlands constituted an example – and, thanks to its temporary and spatially restricted nature, a very graphic one – of the far-reaching process of estrangement in an increasingly abstract world. For Nathan Coley, therefore, this was a perfect opportunity to investigate the architectural, bureaucratic and social manifestations of this process on the basis of an exemplary case. He decided to participate in the Lockerbie trial as an unofficial court artist, observing the trial over four separate periods of time, the longest of which lasted over four weeks. He shared the public gallery with Scottish legal historians and journalists from all over the world; with observers from the United Nations, and relatives of victims and defendants. It resembled an international territory whose atmosphere was dominated by the cultural chasm between the many relatives of the American victims and the relatives of the Libyan defendants. In contrast, the courtroom area – with the Bench, representatives of the Crown, the public prosecutor, the defendants' legal representatives, the defendants themselves, and witnesses – had an unmistakably Scottish character due to its strict Calvinist etiquette and rules of conduct. Coley followed two self-imposed rules during his time in Kamp van Zeist. Firstly, he tried to forget his status as an artist. His main priority was the unbiased observation of the specific situation of the trial and its institutional, logistical and architectural framework. Secondly, he wanted to avoid all contact with relatives of the victims and the defendants. In an interview with Giles Sutherland in *Sculpture Matters* (Issue 13, Scottish Sculpture Trust, Edinburgh 2001), Coley said that it would have served neither his interests nor his function to address the complex question of truth and justice:

Personally I have no connection with the bombing. Emotionally I was horrified by the events. But I didn't think that was my role there. [...] There are other people who can deal with truth.

During the Lockerbie trial, the question of truth and justice was posed from the perspective of the Scottish court. Diverging cultural and philosophical preconditions for 'truth' cannot be taken into consideration by national law courts; their main concern in criminal proceedings is to determine guilt by means of evidence and witnesses' testimony and to punish the crime according to national law, which in turn serves to represent the executive power of the state. Other perspectives, which might make the opinion of the court appear relative, have no place here. In the Lockerbie trial courtroom, the presence of different national, ethnic and professional groups meant that many different points of view on the proceedings were represented – to say nothing of the fact that the case itself was a clear example of fundamentally conflicting political and ideological viewpoints. None of this, however, was relevant to the procedures of the Scottish court, which had to determine the defendants' guilt through circumstantial evidence. Day in and day out, witnesses were summoned to give evidence which might be important for the case. As the proceedings wore on, therefore, Coley came to regard the witness box, placed apart from the other furnishings of the courtroom, as the defining symbol of the Lockerbie trial. This bulky piece of furniture, constructed exclusively for the purpose of questioning witnesses, became for him the focal point of the trial and the Scottish court temporarily instituted at Kamp van Zeist. The very appearance of the witness box was highly significant: its modular architecture – part half-open space, part podium, and looking rather like a desk in a lobby – blended seamlessly with the other fittings of the courtroom and illustrated the bureaucratic, transitory nature of the proceedings.

In 2003, Coley exhibited a work called *Lockerbie* (pp.98–105) in *Days Like These*, Tate Britain's second triennial exhibition of British art. The work consisted of two parts: an exact replica of the original witness box of the Lockerbie trial, and a series of detailed drawings which Coley had made from official press photographs of individual items of evidence (pp.102–105). After his stay in Kamp van Zeist, Coley succeeded in convincing the Imperial War Museum in London to acquire the Lockerbie trial witness box as a highly-charged relic of an extraordinary historical event. Coley decided that the witness box should exist in two separate versions: the original, as a witness to history, and a detailed replica which, on a meta-level, would transfer the ideas and questions relating to the Lockerbie trial to an exhibition context. It is important to note at this point that the replica witness box is a truly exact copy of the original. It was built from the original designs, with identical materials and identical details, and even the signs of wear and tear on the original were reproduced. The imitation actually purports to be the original, thus creating an element of deception which contradicts and even ironically refracts the truth-seeking purpose one associates with witness boxes. The deceptively realistic simulation of this object effectively bears false witness before the observer. Constructing a replica of the original, now in the collection of the Imperial War Museum, was also an act of appropriation that transferred the witness box from the abstract status of public property to the concrete condition of a privately-owned object – a process of appropriation which can also be traced in the act of creating minutely detailed drawings from press photographs.

The question of how to define public and private property, especially from the pluralistic viewpoint of a postmodern society, runs like a continuous thread through all of Nathan Coley's works in widely differing permutations and diverse examples. This question is also a key element of Hannah Arendt's analysis of estrangement in the modern world. According to Hannah Arendt, our personal property is that part of our common world which is privately owned by us; thus the existence and the protection of private property are among the most fundamental political preconditions for human existence on the material level. For the same reason, confiscation is one of the ways in which estrangement manifests itself. Referring to processes of confiscation in the modern age, she argues that at this time not having property meant not having an inherited place in the world – in other words, a person without property was someone for whom the world and its organised political bodies had made no provision. The disastrous consequences which result when groups or individuals lose their inherited place in the world can also be observed in later, and even in recent, examples of confiscation in history: colonialism, the Holocaust, the Chinese occupation of Tibet, and the conflict in the Middle East. The optimistic hypothesis that worldwide liberalisation and the development of a global market economy in the second half of the 20th century would result in an equal distribution of land and wealth was not borne out by events.

In his contribution to the first platform of Documenta11, Stuart Hall summarised what would turn out to be a subtext of Documenta11 as a whole; that pluralisation and fragmentation do not mean that centres of power no longer exist, or that the great inequalities in the distribution of power, resources and privileges that were once subsumed into the general category of 'class' have ceased to exist because the distribution pattern has changed. In most Western societies, the gulf between the haves and the have-nots has widened significantly in the last phase of sustainable economic growth. For Hall, this is a constituent characteristic of Western 'success' – and, naturally, the same tendency can be observed simultaneously on a global scale.

With regard to the Lockerbie trial, the question of property and privilege and the resultant conflict of interests is particularly relevant to the subject of the trial itself: the terrorist attack, which constitutes one of the most radical and distressing modern manifestations of this conflict. There has been much discussion of the fact that, along with an increase in the permeability of national borders, the second half of the 20th century also saw a dramatic increase in nationalist and fundamentalist movements which – especially in recent times – escalated into an alarming number of acts of terrorism. The terrorist attacks on the World Trade Centre on 11 September 2001 were on a greater scale than anything that had been seen before – a scale great enough to change the world order. Referring to Frederic Jameson's recent book on the logic of globalisation, *Globalization and Political Strategy* (Duke University Press, Durham, North Carolina 1998), Stuart Hall views this development as a direct reaction opposing the developments of the modern age. For Hall, many of the variants of nationalism, racism and fundamentalism which have entered the stage of global politics are partly answers – and even acts of opposition – to the constraints of modern globalisation. Not infrequently, they are symptoms of a failed nationalist project under hostile international conditions or of a failed attempt at modernisation.

A case such as the Lockerbie trial shows that the definition of a territorial border can be just as fictional as the legal term implies. It can reach a degree of abstraction that separates the idea of a country's borders from their actual form, with its historical development and concrete shape. However, this kind of abstract construct calls into question any clearly defined concept of national identity and the ensuing claims to territorial sovereignty. It comes as no surprise that Nathan Coley, whose work deals with the relativity of such claims and the complex nature of possible perspectives on the question of sovereignty over a place or a country, should study the phenomenon of terrorism.

In the spring of 2002, Coley was invited by Cube (Centre for Understanding the Built Environment) to participate in the exhibition *Fabrications* organised in Manchester. The exhibition was devoted to the development of the city's structure after the end of the Second World War. Coley produced a work titled *I Don't Have Another Land* (pp.90–91), a model of the former Marks & Spencer building in Manchester which was renowned for its extravagant modernist architecture. With its severely structured façade and dynamic, curving porch canopy, the building was a landmark in the inner city of Manchester for many years and eventually became a kind of secular symbol which significantly shaped the city's identity and became a fixed component of urban memory. In 1997, the much-frequented department store was demolished due to damage inflicted by an IRA bomb. This deprived Manchester not only of a real urban centre, but also of a conceptual one, and the city did not recover from this collective blow until a new building was completed on the site many years later.

Coley visually transferred the melancholy of loss connected to Marks & Spencer's to his sculpture by covering the almost head-height model of the building with a dense layer of matt black pigment that swallows all light and has a velvety texture reminiscent of soot or coal. The model dispenses with the building's interior, the windows, and other details, so that the sculpture resembles the charred skeleton of a heavy dinosaur. Set into the grid of the windowed façade is a series of large letters that resemble text on banners or billboards. The text reads: 'I DON'T HAVE ANOTHER LAND'. Visitors to the exhibition knowing of the IRA terrorist attack will inevitably have presumed this was an IRA slogan. Perversely enough, however, this is not the case. In reality, the text is the title of an Israeli folk song that can be found sprayed as graffiti on walls in Israeli-occupied territories in the Middle East. With this simple line and all the history it implies – a history that ranges back through the Middle East conflict, through the Holocaust, to the Biblical origins of the Jewish people, and which is the history not only of the Jews but of humanity in general – Coley presents at a single stroke all the complexity of the perspectives which are tied inextricably to people's right to identify with a place of community and self-determination. The model of Manchester's Marks & Spencer building which was damaged in the IRA bomb blast illustrates two incompatible worldviews all by itself. But it is the immense complexity and scope of the Middle Eastern conflict that lends the work its full, trenchant impact.

I Don't Have Another Land is a typical work by Nathan Coley in that, like so many of his other works, it uses architecture to reflect political and social questions, and features a building in which individual and collective projections become manifest. Not only was the architecture of the Marks & Spencer building an integral part of the urban identity of the city, but as such it also became a perfect target for the ostentatiously violent expression of the IRA's political demands. However, Coley's interest in the building in Manchester is not confined to the real events that took place there. On a more general level, Coley is also concerned with the visionary quality of the modernist style which, in a metaphorical sense, illustrates how utopias can become real and how architecture can embody ideas. Coley uses the blackened skeleton of the building as an urgent, almost painful reminder of the inconstancy and vulnerability of utopian models.

One of Nathan Coley's earliest works, a public artwork titled *Urban Sanctuary* (pp.26–35), is a very clear example of the artist's interest in architecture and public buildings focusing primarily on the pluralism of perspectives and ideas which they embody. In 1997 Stills Gallery in Edinburgh invited Coley to develop a public artwork during the course of the redevelopment of the gallery by the architects Reiach and Hall. His point of departure was the commission to develop and *improve* a public space by means of a work of art, and he proposed the construction of an urban sanctuary that would be a place of contemplation and transformation: a kind of secularised 'temple' serving two purposes. On the one hand, it would be a place where people in the city could escape conditioning by their urban surroundings. On the other, it would serve as a place of refuge for people who, through government persecution or social disadvantages, have lost their right to a space of their own – or, as Hannah Arendt would say, an inherited place. In this sense it would serve, like Christian sanctuaries in history, as a place exempt from the law. Coley began his project by publicly distributing a notice of his intention to build – a prerequisite for receiving planning permission. Utilising this official procedure seemed to him to be the perfect way to disseminate the idea behind his project, for this was a public announcement for a public work of art. Then Coley consulted a number of specialists – a theologian, an architect, a professional Feng Shui advisor, an artist, an urban planner, a sociologist, a police officer and an assistant at the tourist information centre – in order to determine the architectural, spiritual and social requirements along with the criteria of interior design and urban planning which a building of this sort would need to meet in modern Edinburgh. The diversity of opinions which emerged during these interviews showed that people's ideas of a 'sacred' place of sanctuary were too diverse to arrive at a single *definite* form in today's world. As a result, Coley decided to realise his project not as a building, but as a book in which he would collect and document the many and varied thoughts of the people he had interviewed. The sanctuary itself was never built.

The historical function of a sanctuary was to allow people to 'take refuge with God'. Under the protection of a spiritual place such as a temple, a church, or a monastery – i.e. a place associated with a specific religion – the poor or the persecuted could find a place of refuge. A Christian sanctuary was a place subject not to the secular law of the state, but to the 'higher law of God' before which all people were equal. Criminals could not be arrested within the sacrosanct confines of a Christian sanctuary or a church. Duncan Forrester, a professor of theology whom Nathan Coley interviewed for *Urban Sanctuary* about the history of Christian sanctuaries, reports that this tradition continued in Edinburgh into the 18th century. In these sanctuaries, even people deeply in debt or guilty of serious crimes could find protection and live for long periods of time. Forrester believes that the function of a modern sanctuary is still to give those seeking refuge the same opportunity for inner transformation that is inherent in the traditional concept of a religious sanctuary. However, given today's developments in globalised societies and the social problems created by migration and political persecution, a Christian place of refuge should now place more emphasis on the function of political asylum than was historically the case.

Forrester's idea – deeply rooted in the Christian tradition – of a modern place of sanctuary as a place of transcendence, even without allegiance to a specific faith, is shared by Nicholas Fernée, a professional Feng Shui consultant. Fernée has studied Tibetan Buddhism and is trained to design temples to provide ideal conditions for meditation. He agrees that a modern place of asylum should be a place of transformation and transition: 'a transition from an external environment to an internal environment.' Thus the sanctuary should provide conditions that enable and encourage this transition. Fernée suggests very specific ideas for the appearance of a sanctuary. In contrast, urban planner Stephen Hajducki views the construction of a place of asylum – and any other public

building – primarily as part of a comprehensive urban system. He also believes that even a nightclub or the pub around the corner could constitute a place of sanctuary or refuge in today's world. And the interview with Christine Borland, an artist of Coley's own generation, reveals how subjective expectations of a place of refuge can be today – indeed, Borland believes that this subjectivity is unavoidable. She rejects the idea of a sanctuary that is tied to a religious or political doctrine. As an alternative to a specific, 'sacred' place in the form of a building or monument, she points out the existence of uncategorised, free 'special places' whose function as a place of refuge lies in their personal significance for individuals.

Coley's interview with the police officer, Douglas Kerr, also explicitly confirms that the idea of an asylum exempt from the law under the aegis of a religious organisation is unthinkable in a secular society in which church and state are politically and legally separate. However, in the critical opinion of sociologist Mark Cousins of the Architectural Association in London, the legislation of modern states, which accepts no areas of exemption inside its limits, serves to control all aspects of human existence. And the uncontrollable question of personal belief appears to pose a particular threat to state order. The demands that immigrants and outsiders should become assimilated shows that multicultural society reaches the limits of tolerance when confronted with personal ways of life and forms of belief which deviate from the stipulated canon of values.

The answers to Nathan Coley's questions concerning the form and function of an urban sanctuary in Edinburgh show that spirituality and religion are no longer deeply rooted in people's awareness today. While they may certainly be present – for example, in the case of specialists with a spiritual tradition such as the theologian Duncan Forrester and Feng Shui consultant Nicholas Fernée – they are confined to individuals and no longer have much in common with the prevailing consensus in society. Coley stresses that, when conducting the interviews for *Urban Sanctuary* on the role of spirituality in a secular, enlightened and multi-ethnic society, his primary purpose was not to receive answers, and still less to answer the question himself. What he wanted to do was to probe the pluralistic condition of contemporary society itself and – as in *Lockerbie* and *I Don't Have Another Land* – to show that truth, in such pluralistic societies, is inherently relative. Thus it is in keeping with the immanent logic of the work that Coley did not choose an architectural form representing any concrete notion of an urban sanctuary, but rather that he collected all the viewpoints in a book – a medium which, unlike architecture, circulates freely and does not mark any specific place. The 'space of the text' – as Mark Cousins pointed out with reference to Victor Hugo's theory that, with the invention of the printing press, architecture lost its significance as a conveyor of ideas – 'is somehow everywhere and nowhere.'

Projects /

Lecture

LECTURE IS THE FIRST OF A SERIES OF WORKS MADE TO MIMIC THE FORMAT OF A SLIDE LECTURE. ROWS OF CHAIRS FACE A SCREEN SHOWING IMAGES TAKEN FROM BUILDING AND DEMOLITION SITES AROUND THE CITY OF GLASGOW. THE SOUND OF A WOMAN'S VOICE GIVING A LECTURE ACCOMPANIES THE IMAGES, WHICH CHANGE AUTOMATICALLY EVERY FEW MINUTES.

... / The contrast between the intentional and the accidental is a point of departure for many of Nathan Coley's works. He wants his audience to realise that what we often perceive as designed objects are actually more or less arbitrary and fragile, ideological constructions of a limited value, while what we usually take as being random appearances and objects, more often than we think, are results of intentionally shared culture and aesthetic norms or traditions.

In the slide installation *Lecture*, Coley staged the gallery space as a lecture hall, with a slide projector positioned between rows of chairs showing images from building sites. The slide show was accompanied by a voice-over, sounding convincingly like a credible expert, a designer or an architect, lecturing the audience on the designs, and their underlying intentions. However, as one sat down to look and listen, one soon realised that the message was constantly being contradicted and blurred by the images. Instead of delivering the expected pictures of well-designed buildings and objects, the slides presented 'aesthetic' details of unfinished building sites and houses under repair, as if they were worthy of high esteem. Interestingly, though, the pictures also seem to speak of the postmodern truism that 'ugly is beautiful', thus partially subverting the original irony expressed by the 'double bind' gap between the auditive and the visual aspect of the show. The ripped backsides of the city are still what very many people must accept as an everyday environment, and the definitions of high vs. low culture are questioned. Thus, it is the meaning of designs as cultural objects and signs which Coley seems to be investigating. Being designed (although maybe not according to conventional rules), the (un)designed objects are also (or even more) readable signs of culture.

From
Kari J Brandtzaeg, 'Art, Design and Public Spaces', *Glasgow – A Presentation of the Arts Scene in the 90s*, For Art, Oslo 1998

First 12 slides of 39

1. IN SCALE, THIS IS ONE OF THE SMALLER PROJECTS WE HAVE BEEN INVOLVED IN, I THINK IT'S A GOOD ILLUSTATION OF HOW WE WORK.

2. OUR INITIAL IDEA WAS TO KEEP THE BUTTRESSES QUITE SIMPLE.

3. HAVE THEM RUNNING DIRECTLY OFF THE PAVEMENT, GIVING THEM THIS RATHER OVERSIZED FOOT.

4. AT THE TOP WE HAD THEM SHOOTING UNDER THE EDGE OF THE PANEL.

5. THIS ORANGE MESH MATERIAL WAS ORIGINALLY THOUGHT OF AS SOLELY FUNCTIONAL.

6. ONCE IT WAS INSTALLED IT BECAME SOMETHING QUITE DECORATIVE. REALLY NICE STUFF.

7. IT'S GOOD LOOKING AT IT NOW, THE WAY THE FENCE CURVES INTO THE PAVEMENT, SUBTLY DICTATING HOW THE PUBLIC MOVE ROUND IT.

8. IT'S QUITE SIMILAR TO OTHER PROJECTS WE'VE DONE - ITS USE OF NATURAL MATERIALS AND VERY LITTLE USE OF COLOUR.

9. OK. THIS NEXT ONE IS OF A JOB WE DID EARLIER IN THE YEAR, TO IN SOME WAY SORT OUT WHAT WAS HAPPENING ON THIS WALL.

10. WE FELT IT NEEDED TO BE HUMANISED, KIND OF MARKED... THIS IS WHAT WE CAME UP WITH.

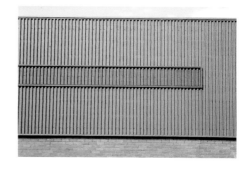

11. THIS IS JUST A DETAIL.

12. THE SHADOW OF THE STREET LAMP IS KIND OF NICE AS WELL... WELL IT APPEALS TO ME.

Urban Sanctuary

URBAN SANCTUARY IS A PUBLIC ARTWORK IN THE FORM OF A BOOK. INVITED TO COLLABORATE WITH ARCHITECTS REIACH AND HALL ON THEIR REDEVELOPMENT OF STILLS GALLERY IN EDINBURGH, COLEY PRODUCED THIS BOOK OF INTERVIEWS WHICH DOCUMENT THE ARTIST'S ATTEMPT TO ESTABLISH A PUBLIC SANCTUARY IN EDINBURGH.

... / Nathan Coley's involvement in the redevelopment of Stills Gallery was part of the 'art for architecture' initiative administered by the Royal Society for the encouragement of Arts Manufacturing and Commerce in London. The scheme sought to involve artists from the very beginning of an architectural process, questioning the ideas and processes leading up to an architectural solution rather than merely placing art in a finished building.

Coley's response to the brief for the project was predicated on the realisation that a building exists within the minds of those with a stake in its making long before it is designed, let alone built. A member of the project team, Coley had access to everyone working on the remaking of Stills, and produced a work which responds to the aspirational and conceptual processes involved. Taking on the role of client, Coley imagined what it would be to commission a new building for Edinburgh. *Urban Sanctuary* is a document of the conversations that might impact on the development of a brief for the new building – a sanctuary, rich in mental associations. Never intending actually to build the building, Coley explored the processes involved in believing

that he might, in interviews with a theologian, an architect, a Feng Shui consultant, an artist, an urban planner, an architectural sociologist, a policeman and the Edinburgh Tourist Information Centre.

The interviews were published in a book, the very particular typographic style of which emphasised the importance of intangible activities like talking and thinking – moving ideas around – to the obviously tangible process of building a building. A copy of the book was placed in every public library in Edinburgh.

Project brief
The artist will be asked to produce a permanent or temporary artwork as part of the wider development of Stills Gallery in Edinburgh. The work must refer to the building and/or the processes applied to develop the site. If the work is intended to be temporary then a record of the work must be made which is available to the public for a minimum of two years. The selected artist could consider a range of processes involved in the redevelopment of Stills, the collaborations associated with all aspects of the building's transformation, and the public's potential to engage with this period of transition and its final outcome.

1.
Mark **Cousins**
Architectural Association, London

THE QUESTION OF UGLINESS.

1.

The deal here at the Architectural Association is I give 25 lectures on something different every year. The question of sanctuary came up in one year's set of lectures which were actually an attempt to think about the question of ugliness. It came up as a reconsideration of the Victor Hugo novel **Notre-Dame de'Paris**, in which one of the questions Hugo asks is what makes a building alive or dead. He gives some famous answers to why a building like Notre Dame is, in his view, dead. One reason is because of all the alterations that have been made to it since the fifteenth century, all of which have been made by architects and any buildings that are made by architects are automatically dead as far as Victor Hugo is concerned. The second reason, which is perhaps a more surprising one, is that architecture for him is killed off by the printing press. What he means by that is that in the Middle Ages ideas circulated largely in the form of stone - stone buildings. That the culture of the community was formulated and expressed in and as building and that at the moment ideas begin to be expressed as texts they occupy a different kind of space. The space of the text is somehow everywhere and nowhere.

2.
It's in your imagination.

1.
Yes. The fact that it is in a pamphlet is neither here nor there, and it is certainly no longer localised as a building materialised in stone.

But there is a third reason which the secondary literature doesn't seem to take any notice of [perhaps because they think it is a bit vulgar] which is the question of Quasimodo and his relation to Notre-Dame. Now it is clear first of all that Quasimodo is too ugly to be in society and he is actually found at a particular part of the west door of Notre-Dame where people abandon those things or people who are not wanted. Four or five religious women find him and are startled by his absolute hideousness. He is taken into the cathedral by the Deacon, Archdeacon Frollo and, as is well known, he later becomes a bell ringer. A lot of the novel is devoted to showing the curious symbiotic relation between the body of Quasimodo and the body of the cathedral. At one level it is almost as if the cathedral is a kind of maternal body in which, however hideous he is, he has finally found a safe space. At the end of the novel Quasimodo abandons the cathedral and prostrates himself before the dead body of the gypsy girl Esmeralda. At that point Victor Hugo says, to those who really know, the cathedral stopped breathing. Now, when people talk about sanctuary with respect of the novel it is normally Esmeralda that they think of as having found a kind of sanctuary, but it seems to me that Quasimodo does also.

Of course in terms of the history and politics of sanctuary, what sanctuary really means is that there is an overlapping of legal jurisdictions, so that for example the interiors of churches, in so far as they are organised and run by ecclesiastical law, are not subject to secular law.

As far as I can see, what you could say is that what happens legally is that the rise of the modern state is precisely a form of the rule of law which permits no space to be outside its legislation. So in legal terms I have no doubt that people would say there is no such thing as sanctuary, certainly not in a country like the UK where the church and state are mutually identified. I think it's quite interesting almost as a comment or as a footnote on the whole question of sanctuary. Why is it that a modern state treats almost as one of its foremost ambitions the wish to abolish any space within its own territory which is not saturated with its own legal force and power. You could say in a sense modern judicial space seeks to exhaust the whole territory to the point that from the seventeenth and eighteenth century onwards you have very comic effects where the law makes it very clear [although it is supposed to believe in God] that God is undoubtedly subordinate in legal terms. There is a famous case of an entire village in Haute Savoie called Modseine which had regularly been the site of miracles and magical practices, things that would now be sociologically called social outbreaks of mass hysteria. Where in the seventeenth century a large notice was put up saying "There will be no miracles here, by order of the King" just to show that modern legal space considers itself actually superior even to the idea of God having any space. Probably the only space in modern society which remains equivocal is literally the physical space of sovereignty itself.

2.
What do you mean by space of sovereignty?

1.
Well there are very weird spatial considerations about the Palace of Westminster precisely because it cannot be subject to the law because it is the source of law.

1. cont. SO I BELIEVE, FOR EXAMPLE, NO-ONE IS ALLOWED TO DIE IN THE PALACE OF WESTMINSTER, THEY HAVE TO BE DRAGGED OUT. NO-ONE CAN FORMALLY BE ARRESTED IN THE PALACE. AS I RECALL THIS USED TO BE EXPLOITED VERY BEAUTIFULLY IN THE EARLY SEVENTIES WHEN YOUNG RESEARCHERS THERE REALISED THAT THE PALACE OF WESTMINSTER WAS CERTAINLY **THE BEST PLACE IN LONDON TO DEAL DRUGS** BECAUSE THERE WAS NO POSSIBILITY OF BEING ARRESTED. THE ONLY SPACE LEFT AS IT WERE UNREGULATED BY THE LAW IS THE VERY SPACE OF THE FORMULATION OF LAW.

2.

What is nice thinking back to Victor Hugo's thoughts about a building dying or living is if we think of bricks and mortar creating not only physical space but also mental and legal space.

1.

It seems to me that what is interesting about the idea of sanctuary and actually I think it's what is valuable about the idea [although we no longer have the reality of it] is that it is as, it were, a space that accepts one unconditionally: that is to say there is no form of recognition or price which is required to be admitted. It's the idea of being accepted completely without being judged and in a sense being protected at least within that space from the force of judgement that would apply to you if you were outside that space. As such it's a very, very valuable idea because almost all the spaces we can think of in a kind of rationalised modern society, you are there because of some right of membership because you are already X or Y and therefore have the right of entry. Questions of for example passports, of the status of immigrants, all the issues of traversing borders, you have to have the right to go in, in order to pass, or they are forms of entry which you purchase as a commodity and therefore have rights within a space. In California at the moment you have shopping malls which may simulate what we used to call public spaces but in fact in order to get into them you have to present a valid credit card. That doesn't mean that you are charged, it's simply that you have to be a subject of credit. And of course those spaces are not only becoming much larger [relative to what we would have called public space] but it's a simple political and legal fact that the American constitution for example doesn't run in these private spaces. So you might try and make a shopping mall look like a public space, but within it you have no freedom of speech, no freedom of assembly, no freedom to distribute literature, etc. none of the constitutional rights.

2.

I'm just thinking what someone like Richard Sennett would make of that, in terms of the Fall of Public Man.

1.

I think for Richard that would simply be another index of, not so much the fragmentation of spaces, but the disillusion of public space where public space is considered to be at one and the same time somewhere where people can freely congregate but as it were that notion of congregation immediately has a political force in which people can organise articulate desires and demands and can use the space as a political medium.

2.

It brings to mind that idea that the most important part of the city is not necessarily the buildings and the frameworks that contain people, it's much more the spaces in-between these things.

1.

Well, I think that's right. Now I dare say that over the last few years in France and in England there have been occasions where politically people have actually exploited the space of churches quite interestingly to in a sense resist arrest, frequently around issues of immigration, to shame the public authorities from rushing into churches and arresting people on so called sacred ground and even though there isn't any legal basis for sanctuary there still obviously is a kind of symbolic.

2.

It's the notion that the police have to enforce law by consent. It is very difficult for them to enforce laws which the mass of the community would be against.

1.

Well I think you have two different views. Interventionist and foolish police forces often say their task is the suppression of crime, but that overlooks a whole kind of tradition. One can put it in the language which was actually very well expressed in Lord Scarman's report into the disturbances in Brixton where he was the first for a very long time to remind people in a judicial capacity that the function of the police was to maintain the Queen's peace. Now, he may have put it in these rather archaic terms but clearly if the function of the police is to maintain peace in the community and on the streets it is clear that their first task is not the detection of crime and the arrest of criminals but that may well be in certain circumstances diametrically opposed to the other constraint of keeping the peace. Alternatively you will always find the senior police saying their task is to enforce things like drug laws, but actually there is a very good judicial argument that that is not their first and not their only task to the point where the police themselves become a threat to public order they are clearly in violation of their original function.

1.
Mark Cousins
Architectural Sociologist

2.
Nathan Coley

THIS IDEA OF SANCTUARY REALLY STRIKES AT THE HEART OF A CERTAIN LIBERAL IDEA OF SOCIETY.

1. cont.

I think it is useful to think of the ways in which in a rationalised society there is a need for sanctuary. One arena in which there is a very strong need is in mental health. We have seen over the last fifteen years a Government-led policy to massively close down mental hospitals without any real corresponding resources going into an alternative policy of what is laughably called 'care in the community'. As a consequence one can see a large number of people on the streets who are in desperate need of some form of sanctuary. It doesn't mean to say that you have a medically utopian view of what psychiatry might be able to do or achieve. It's rather that people will frequently over the period of their life need somewhere especially outside the family and especially not out on the street to go. Somewhere that will accept them unconditionally and where they will be free of the normal responsibilities.

2.

Yes. The individual needs sanctuary from the pressures of normal [whatever that is] life. But also on some occasions the community needs sanctuary from the individual. The extreme of that is that we imprison people who commit crimes.

1.

Well, I think that is stretching language. There seems to be a different problem to why we incarcerate and enclose people . I am not suggesting that there is any easy alternative to it. But I think it is worth retaining for the idea of sanctuary that it is something that you voluntarily seek and in a sense that you can leave sanctuary. Of course as always the rich know this perfectly well and devised all sorts of ways for achieving sanctuary at a price. This idea of sanctuary really strikes at the heart of a certain liberal idea of society. If a liberal society is based almost on the idea of a contract in which citizens have mutually implicated sets of responsibilities and rights, that's all very well but there is something about

society, something more fundamental than that which is to say I accept you as shall we say a human being long before I accept you as a citizen, but in accepting you as a human being I don't have any rights, you don't owe me anything as a consequence of that recognition. It's part of a structure of the unconditional right - sorry, the unconditional recognition - of another human being from which flow no rights, no responsibilities on the part of the person that is recognised but in which obligations do flow from me having recognised you as a human being there are certain things you have an unconditional right to.

2.

How do you think that sits alongside the needs of the late capitalist environment in terms of the make-up of the city and what it demands from its citizens?

1.

Well, the late capitalist city isn't doing too well on its own: it's not doing too well by privatising space, it's not doing too well by trying to substitute security for safety. Its cities are sometimes being turned into a kind of distopian nightmare, especially for the poor. So it seems to me that to begin to open out some of these questions, [however utopian they might seem] - it's not that we could suddenly invent and materialise a number of spaces of sanctuary which would be popularly regarded as a kind of threat to decent ordered values, but it has something to do with the fact that at the moment we are at least at an urban level losing that primary recognition of other humans' right to exist unless they can be the bearers of certain responsibilities and obligations. So it's not accidental that the idea of sanctuary has a certain medieval, a certain religious origin not because its re-application would be anarchistic or indeed religious but one finds the term really arising in a sense before a certain liberal rationalisation of social relations.

2.

Do you think the need for sanctuary is different from what it was?

1.

I think it is greater because if you think about it historically one thing which you could do in pre-modern societies, with those who are so called outwith the community, you could outlaw them. Clearly you had judgements of banishment or the imposition of exile.

2.

Outwith the city walls?

1.

That's right, which of course was just a medieval equivalent of 'not in my back yard'. People developed things like a 'ship of fools' where they would put disturbed people on a ship and just float them down river. With a more rationalised urban society the major spatial change has been since the seventeenth century with the increasing idea of not the banishment but the enclosure of those that are a threat. An enclosure in a range of institutions and obviously we owe a lot to the work of Michael Foucault in articulating them. Institutions which at first were there to banish citizens internally, no longer to push them out but to draw them within set walls.

2.

Was that because of industrialisation and the need for more space due to the growth of the city?

1.

Well I think it was the outcome of a number of complex sets of relations. One was certainly to deal with the threat or the reality of widespread petty crime. Obviously in the development of national markets in the seven-teenth and eighteenth centuries the kind of thing that threatens the commercialisation of a society are things like petty theft - pilfering. Now at first the draconian answer was 'we'll just hang 'em all', but in the eighteenth century where there were jury systems, jurors were less and less ready to pronounce a verdict of guilt, and across Roman law societies a generation of reformers thought this was a bit draconian. The question at the end of the eighteenth century was, 'how do you begin to develop ways of punishing people with less than death'. It is very difficult for us to recover the sheer strangeness, the sheer novelty of the idea of prison and the rapidity with which it caught on in every society. So there we have a notion of enclosure, which to some extent was generalised also to lunatic asylums and to some extent even schools and so we don't really have an alternative spatial organisation so again maybe sanctuary, although it has these pre-modern origins, is something that still has a future in front of it.

Essentially, the modern state has a notion of territory and a notion effectively of space. All space must be dominated by it's law. Hence we can see the incredible anxiety with which the state looks at the development of cyberspace because one of the things that immediately raises its concerns is that it is a space which it is very difficult to dominate legally. So it may well be that at least intellectually, one could even make a case for saying the internet constitutes a form of intellectual sanctuary or may do or whatever. It seems to me that it is easy to overstate the political radicalism of cyberspace but what is interesting is the way in which governments speak only really on how to bring this new space under proper legal regulation. Legal systems abhor an unregulated space.

Villa Savoye

VILLA SAVOYE MAKES ITS MEANING THROUGH THE JUXTAPOSITION OF A SET OF IMAGES TAKEN OF AN ORDINARY HOUSE IN A CONTEMPORARY HOUSING DEVELOPMENT AND A 'LECTURE' WHICH IS A COMPILATION OF TEXTS WRITTEN ABOUT ONE OF THE MOST FAMOUS, ICONIC BUILDINGS IN ARCHITECTURAL HISTORY, LE CORBUSIER'S VILLA SAVOYE.

... / Presenting a lecture, the installation mimics a persistent reality. Firmly rooted in the real, its screen and chairs seem at home in the space they have claimed in the gallery, its subjects suitably visual and appropriately mediated for exhibition as art. Immediately, however, the installation as art denies the extreme materiality of its presentation. The house we see – a newly-built suburban house – comes to us on slide, the most ephemeral of photographic media. Pure projected light, the images are in perpetual motion away from both the house as real object and the photograph as 'real' artwork. Similarly the house we hear – Le Corbusier's Villa Savoye – denies us both its actual presence and the presence of its creator or even its describer.

What we are faced with is the presentation of a sequence of codes which seem to be conforming to the activity of mimesis, to be attempting to order the world within a securely grounded system of coherence and intelligibility, but which are instead slipping away from such a system, determinedly undermining the very security they apparently offer. The codes are familiar: as contemporary viewers we think we know what this type of new house looks like, and which particular

sets of aspirations and cultural and architectural presentations it represents. As gallery goers we are probably conversant with the rhetoric (and the sights and sounds) of the slide lecture. As an audience of art we may well be aware of at least the existence if not the iconic status of the Villa Savoye. What we do not already know we can of course learn. The installation conceals nothing and, sitting easily through its entire loop, we can, on a second .viewing, add recognition to remembrance. The work connects with us twice – once as individuals outside its sphere of influence but open to it, and once (if we accept the invitation to watch it through) as favoured intimates, a 'smart' audience complicit with its systems of representation.

What it actually does, of course, is disconnect with us. It articulates a disconcerting and amusing lack of fit which is announced in the preliminary disjunction between the suburban house and the Villa Savoye, continued in every element of the presentation (the chairs are not ones we would expect in the context of the other gallery furniture; the voice, being female, cannot be the expected architect, author or artist) and affects not only how we experience the installation but also how we subsequently address ourselves to the rest of the world around us. The installation, which presents itself as fact is, in fact, really fiction or, more precisely, a sequence of fictions. It manipulates a network of expected resemblances which are from the first illusory, each part in the network failing to connect with the next so that the network itself

becomes a signal of its own disinclination actually to represent the world (or perhaps its inclination to misrepresent it). The work is constructed to be haunted by the signs of likeness, characterised by a drive towards some desired absolute which guarantees likeness but which ends only in the reality of the artist. He, as author and editor of the piece, creator and manipulator of the fiction is the origin of the chain of illusory resemblance and representation. But he, like the 'home' behind the slides and the architectural classic beneath the descriptions, is not actually there.

From
Fiona Bradley, 'Homing In',
Correspondences,
Scottish National Gallery of
Modern Art, Edinburgh 1998

THE SITE IS EXPANSIVE, BORDERED BY TREES ON THREE SIDES, AND HAS LONG VIEWS TOWARDS THE SOFT ROLLING FIELDS AND VALLEY.

THE GRAVEL TURNS SLOWLY INTO THE TREES, ITS DESTINATION UNKNOWN.

AT FIRST SIGHT, THERE IS A SHOCK OF RECOGNITION A SENSE OF FORMAL INEVITABILITY. WHAT COULD BE MORE NATURAL THAN THIS HORIZONTAL WHITE BOX, POISED ON PILLARS, SET OFF AGAINST THE RURAL SURROUNDINGS, THE FAR PANORAMA AND THE SKY?

ON THE SIDE OF THE BUILDING, PILLARS ARE FLUSH WITH THE FAÇADE, GIVING A CLEAR READING OF LOAD AND SUPPORT.

BIT BY BIT YOU GATHER THAT THE VILLA IS NOT AS DETACHED AS IT FIRST APPEARS.

IT IS SCULPTED AND HOLLOW TO ALLOW THE SURROUNDINGS TO ENTER IT.

"A house as a machine for living in"

Pigeon Lofts

PIGEON LOFTS IS A SLIDE
INSTALLATION IN WHICH IMAGES OF
THE LOFTS PIGEON-FANCIERS BUILD
TO HOUSE THEIR BIRDS ARE
PROJECTED TOGETHER WITH A
VOICE-OVER DESCRIBING A RANGE
OF PRODUCTS – THE TONE
SUGGESTS CONSERVATORIES,
HOUSE EXTENSIONS OR UP-MARKET
SUMMER HOUSES.

... / Nathan Coley has given his
work the appearance of an audio-
visual presentation, like those to
be found, for instance, at trade
fairs: a slide projection with
professionally spoken, taped
commentary, a screen and chairs.
By referring to a style of
presentation used for information
and instruction purposes, Nathan
Coley attempts to withdraw his
projection from the fetishisation
process surrounding the image in
the context of art. This is in fact
the reason why he does not, for
instance, simply hang framed
photographs on the wall. This
discursive element of the work is
not just to be found in the form of
its mediation, but could be said to
be at its very centre. It is a work of
documentation, information and
reflection.

39 slides photographed by
Nathan Coley are projected in
succession. In close up and in
long shots, photographed in
various ways, they show pigeon
lofts found in the Glasgow area,
constructed by local inhabitants,
without planning permission or
architectural instruction, and using
available, second-hand or found
materials. All these constructions
are different from each other. They
reflect the skill, pretensions,
imagination, and care of their
builders and show what materials
are available. They are unique

entities. Aesthetic considerations,
though, seem to have played no
part in their construction. On the
other hand there is a whole
series of features, based on
functional requirements, which the
individual constructions have in
common: the tower shape, the
high position of the entrance
accessible by ladder, the lack of
windows, the distance from
human dwellings, etc.

The projection of the slides is
accompanied by a pleasant yet
neutral voice, commenting on
each image in such a way as to
give the impression that the
objects shown are the products of
some firm and are being
presented to potential customers.
The actual purpose of these
constructions, though, is not
made apparent in the
presentation: it is limited to the
general rhetoric concerning the
proposed advantages, opinions,
usefulness and status of the
various models, all camouflaged
as information.

The photographic
documentation of these individual
and anonymous constructions,
which are functionally orientated
according to improvised
construction methods ('bricolage',
Claude Levy-Strauss) but devoid
of stylistic considerations,
obviously contains many art-
historical references. The clearest
connection is with Bernd and Hilla
Becher's photographic project of
Anonymous Sculptures, though in
Nathan Coley's photographs
neither such strictness of method
nor such photographic isolation of
the subject are attempted. Like
the Bechers, Coley proposes to
consider these objects within the
context of public sculpture. [...]
The decisive difference between

Coley's work and that of Bernd
and Hilla Becher, though, is that
his first step is to use a spoken
commentary as a framework for
the photographs and only
secondly does he put them into an
art context. This commentary,
then, contradicts all the
characteristics of the pigeon lofts
themselves: these anonymous
constructions are passed off as
elements in some unspecified
firm's range of models, the
individually produced structures
are presented as being
commercially mass-produced, and
something quite lacking in stylistic
and aesthetic features is passed
off as the outcome of specific
prestige-laden formal
commitments. What is noticeably
absent in the commentary is any
statement about the function of
these structures, which is, on the
other hand, announced in the
overall title of the work: pigeon
lofts. If, however, this advertising
message, which point for point
misrepresents the reality of the
structures documented by Nathan
Coley, is seen as the presentation
of a range of sculptures in public
spaces, it functions as an ironic
commentary on the assumptions
inherent in this field.

From
Ulrich Loock, 'Mutual
Contextualization', Glasgow,
Kunsthalle Bern, Bern 1997

THIS IS OUR STANDARD MODEL,
INCORPORATING CORRUGATED IRON,
STEEL SHEETING AND REINFORCED
PLYWOOD.

WHAT IS ILLUSTRATED HERE IS OUR
UNIQUE SEPARATION DESIGN BETWEEN
THE LOWER GROUND LEVEL SECTION
AND THE UPPER LEVEL.

THIS IS ONE OF OUR NEWEST LINES.

THIS SHOT SHOWS THE THREE-LAYER
CONSTRUCTION, GIVING YOU
DURABILITY, STRENGTH AND AN
ATTRACTIVE APPEARANCE.

SEEN HERE, SINGLE STANDING, THIS
IS 30% HIGHER THAN MOST, GIVING
YOU A LITTLE EXTRA HEIGHT WHERE
REQUIRED.

THIS IS AN OLD FAVOURITE.

Demolition in Progress

DEMOLITION IN PROGRESS WAS
PART OF A PROJECT CALLED *BLIND
DATE*, IN WHICH PAIRS OF ARTISTS
WERE INVITED TO MEET IN A
SPECIFIC SITE TO DEVELOP INTER-
RELATED WORKS. COLEY WAS
INTRODUCED TO THE ARTIST
THOMAS BECHINGER AND OFFERED
THE SITE OF THE PAVILLON DER
VOLKSBÜHNE ON ROSA-
LUXEMBURG-PLATZ IN BERLIN.

... / NC In terms of our
collaboration, I think Thomas
and my practices are very
different from each other. As a
painter, Thomas has a studio-
based practice. My work,
however, is mostly related to
context. The connotations of the
materials which we were going to
introduce into our collaboration at
the Pavilion have totally different
histories. All that we had done
before we met was the laying
down of our general ideas about
what we planned to do with the
Pavilion: Thomas had the idea of
painting on the windows, i.e.
changing the windows by putting
paint on them, and I wanted to
disfunctionalise the building by
demolishing it and using a fence
as material. Both approaches
made the space into an object
rather than using the space as a
site for work. This made the work
an event rather than an exhibition.

TB We were departing from two
different directions and we met
somewhere in between. I came
from the inside of the Pavilion
painting directly on the
architecture and Nathan came
from the outside. He was
reinterpreting the Pavilion. So we
met not in the building, but on its
surface. Between the building and
the fence.

NC I was quite conscious that
Thomas wasn't going to use the
walls, that he was going to use
the glass, and I guess my
proposal to demolish the Pavilion,
was to demolish the difficult
context in which Thomas was
going to find himself. With the
fence we haven't introduced a
new language to Berlin. These
fences are everywhere. I have
rather appropriated a very
common language. With the idea
of demolishing the Pavilion I was
certainly commenting on the
transition and the possibilities that
Berlin has at the moment. But it
has also to do with the notion that
a creative act can be to take away
rather than to add.

TB With the information we
received from the demolition
company we became aware of
what it means to demolish a
building. For example, how the
procedure of demolition is usually
structured and that all material is
going to be selected and
completely recycled. It also
showed the difference between
our concept of demolishing the
Pavilion, and what a demolition
company does. For example, how
differently a demolition company
would install a fence around a
building. Here at the Pavilion, we
installed the fence very close to
the building. It is much more
framing the building than fencing
it off.

NC The sign is very important. It
works as a headline as well as
underlining the concept. It directs
the audience not to look at the
fence, the painting and the lights
only in a formal sense. It is
ambiguous; on the one hand it is a
piece of public information and on

the other hand it cannot be
misread as being a sign on a
building site. It has the wrong
colours, the wrong design, the
wrong location.

TB For me the sign is the 'real'
piece of art in this installation.
The way in which we discussed
the sign – what material we would
use, which kind of letters and
colour – we entered the history of
art again. The paintings are not
paintings, I just added paint on the
windows, and the way that Nathan
used the fence, he did not
transform the fence into a
sculpture. But the sign is a piece
of art.

From
A conversation between Thomas
Bechinger, Nathan Coley, Susanne
Gaensheimer and Maria Lind,
Blind Date, Munich 1998

Minster

THE LAST OF COLEY'S SLIDE
LECTURE WORKS, *MINSTER*
PRESENTS THREE SPACES
SIMULTANEOUSLY. THE SLIDES
DOCUMENT A NONCONFORMIST
CHAPEL IN TOXTETH, LIVERPOOL.
THE LECTURE IS TAKEN FROM THE
PUBLIC GUIDED TOUR OF YORK
MINSTER. THE ACCOMPANYING
EXPLANATORY PAMPHLET DETAILING
THE CORRECT PROCEDURE FOR
ESTABLISHING A TABERNACLE OR
PORTABLE SANCTUARY, USES TEXT
FROM *THE SYNAGOGUE* BY
H A MEEK, 1995.

... / As part of the exhibition
Artranspennine98, Nathan Coley
was invited to make a work for the
new top floor gallery of Tate
Gallery Liverpool, a space that
had been lying dormant since the
conversion of the rest of the
building from bonded warehouse
to art gallery in 1988. First
experienced by the artist as an
empty warehouse on top of a
national art collection, it exerted a
powerful influence on his
understanding of Tate Gallery
Liverpool. The challenge
presented by *Artranspennine98*
was to site in this newly converted
gallery work which was in some
way revelatory of its dual identity.
In inviting Nathan Coley and five
other artists to place work in this
context, the curators hoped to
engage with the ways in which
spaces and the objects they
house are structured and
restructured in dialogue with the
inhabitants and audiences they
attract.
  Coley's work was installation-
based and allusively site-specific,
regularly using the familiar rhetoric
of a slide lecture to stage a
particular interaction between
audience and place. *Minster*

presented three spaces, all
exterior to the gallery and all
hovering, like the phantom
warehouse which haunts Tate
Gallery Liverpool, between reality
and remembrance. Projected
slides documented a
Nonconformist chapel in Toxteth,
Liverpool. An accompanying
recorded lecture took us on a
guided tour of York Minster. An
explanatory pamphlet set out the
correct procedure for establishing
a tabernacle or portable
sanctuary. The piece was
characteristically didactic, and yet
its message was entirely open: the
images were neutral and
unmediated slides; the voice was
recorded and clearly that of an
actress; the text was excerpted,
its authorial voice separated from
its original context.
  The photographed, recorded
and written spatial descriptions
were presented as though
illustrative of one another. The lack
of fit between them (the images
showed a plain window just as the
guide was extolling the wonders
of York Minster's stained glass)
were amusing and disruptive, yet
pointed, paradoxically, to an
underlying similarity. Though they
seemed to be on a mission to
explain, none of the descriptions
was actually about the place to
which it related. Rather they
described an intimate experience
of place – one, however differently
expressed, rooted in belief, pride
and a sense of familiarity with
convention. The spaces were all
revealed as elaborate fictions,
constructed and experienced
according to a strict set of rules
(of adornment, of plainness, of
procedure). In Tate Gallery
Liverpool, the work was revelatory
of the way in which audiences as

well as architects structure
spaces; the way in which our
experience of a place is inevitably
its reality.

From
Fiona Bradley, 'Nathan Coley,
Minster', *Artranspennine98*,
August Media, London 1999

THIS IS SAINT STEPHEN'S CHAPEL AND IS DEDICATED TO HEALING AND
PEACE, AND SERVICES ARE SAID REGULARLY HERE. THE MEMORIALS ON THE
WALLS ARE TO THE MEN OF MEDICINE, AND YOU HAVE A CARVING OF
'HYGEIA', THE GODDESS OF MEDICINE. THERE IS ALSO A LITTLE BUST OF
MOTHER TERESA. I THINK IF PEOPLE ARE FEELING VERY CONCERNED FOR
SOMEONE IT MUST BE VERY COMFORTING TO COME AND SIT HERE AND SEND
UP A FEW PRAYERS ...

THE HIGH ALTAR. REMEMBER THIS IS THE HEART OF THE CATHEDRAL. BEFORE THERE WAS SEATING IN THE NAVE, THIS IS WHERE THE PRAISE ALWAYS WENT AND STILL CONTINUES. A LOT OF PEOPLE NOW WORSHIP AT THE MINSTER, BUT IN THOSE DAYS THERE WERE ALL THE LITTLE PARISH CHURCHES SO YOU ONLY HAD PROBABLY THE PRIESTS IN THIS AREA.

NOT EVERYTHING IN THE MINSTER WAS MADE FOR THE MINSTER. THE CROSS
IS SPANISH 16TH CENTURY AND WAS ACQUIRED, AND WE LOVE IT BECAUSE
IT EMBELLISHES AND ENRICHES US. AND I THINK IT'S VERY NICE TO
THINK THAT SOMEBODY IN SPAIN MADE THAT IN THE 16TH CENTURY AND WE
NOW HAVE IT IN THE MINSTER. SO THAT'S THE HIGH ALTAR.

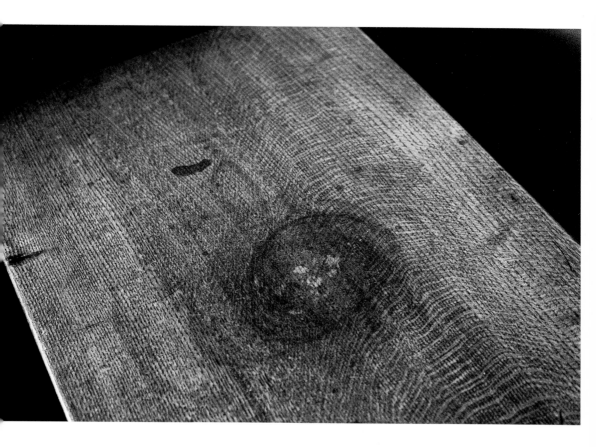

A Public Announcement

THIS PROJECT WAS ORIGINALLY EXHIBITED IN TWO PARTS. THE SERIES OF EIGHT SCREEN PRINTS, EACH BEARING THE WORDS OF A HISTORICAL PUBLIC ANNOUNCEMENT, WERE EXHIBITED TOGETHER WITH EIGHT PHOTOGRAPHS OF URBAN PUBLIC SPACES AND A SOUND RECORDING OF AN ACTOR READING OUT THE PROCLAMATIONS. FOLLOWING THE EXHIBITION, THE PRINTED ANNOUNCEMENTS APPEARED IN ROTATION ON A PUBLIC POSTER SITE.

... / Nathan Coley has translated existent texts that proclaim authority over land or space into large screen printed posters as part of this specially commissioned project for The Changing Room. The appeal of the original words, which would often have been spoken by a town crier, is their universality and sense of politics. Their relationship to Stirling as a historical town is not direct but implicit and, as such, timeless.

THERE WILL BE
NO MIRACLES HERE.
BY ORDER OF THE KING

TURN BACK. YOU ARE
GOING THE WRONG WAY.

NO ACCESS BEYOND THIS
POINT WITHOUT
POSSESSION.

AS IT IS INDESPENSABLY
NECESSARY THAT
FAMILIES SHOULD LEAVE
THIS TOWN. THEY MUST
PREPARE TO EMBARK
FOR SUCH PLACES AS
SHALL BE DECIDED.
BY ORDER DEPUTY ADJUTANT GENERAL

GENTLEMEN. IMPROPER
SHOWS AND EXHIBITIONS
IN THE MARKET PLACE
ARE FORBIDDEN.
AS OF AND FROM 3RD SEPTEMBER

THIS VILLAGE AND
SURROUNDING
HEATHLAND IS PRIVATE
PROPERTY.

PERSONS CREATING A
NOISE OR DISTURBANCE,
IN OR NEAR THIS PUBLIC
STREET ARE GUILTY OF
A MISDEMEANOUR AND
ARE LIABLE TO FINE AND
IMPRISONMENT.

ANY PERSON WILFULLY
INJURING ANY PART OF
THIS COUNTY BRIDGE
WILL BE GUILTY OF
FELONY AND UPON
CONVICTION LIABLE TO
BE TRANSPORTED FOR
LIFE.
BY THE COURT

The eight text panels are presented framed in oak, behind glass. The recorded voice of a man reading the texts fills the gallery. Extricated from their original context, the texts are highly ambiguous and full of meaning.

Through this deconstruction, space is created; space for us to consider the meaning of these phrases. Who uttered these words and why? Walking around the gallery reading the texts, the interruptions of the actor's received pronunciation repeating the statements at regular intervals, brings more sharply into focus the notions of authority to which the whole work alludes.

Colour photographs of diverse

spaces all marked by some form of discrete or explicit control are interspersed between texts: Central Station in Glasgow, The Craigs in Stirling, the back court of a tenement block.

The idea of place is a complex one within the work. It refers to place as somewhere information flows in and around. It refers specifically to public squares as well as place of exhibition; where the artwork is seen, where it functions, is understood and remembered. The final stage of *A Public Announcement* is the return of the texts to the public realm. Each text will be sited in a specifically located poster site for one month. Without instruction or accreditation, or the context of the gallery space, the ambiguity of the text will draw on the environment in which they are read.

The text panel, although visually fragile, is a mighty work. It expresses in a slight gesture the complex relationship between art, the gallery and what constitutes its audience. It does all this at the same time as addressing its theme; that of how authority is exercised in public space.

From
Jackie Shearer, *Nathan Coley – A Public Announcement*,
The Changing Room, Stirling 1998

THERE WILL BE
NO MIRACLES HERE.

BY ORDER OF THE KING

A Manifesto for Bournville

THIS PHOTOGRAPH WAS MADE AS PART OF *IN THE MIDST OF THINGS*, AN EXHIBITION OF SITE-SPECIFIC ARTISTS' COMMISSIONS IN BOURNVILLE, THE VILLAGE CREATED OUTSIDE BIRMINGHAM IN 1895 BY THOMAS CADBURY, THE QUAKER PHILANTHROPIST AND CHOCOLATE FACTORY OWNER, TO HOUSE THE WORKERS FROM HIS CHOCOLATE FACTORY. COLEY'S PHOTOGRAPH WAS SITED IN AN UNUSED UNDERPASS.

... / Nathan Coley's project was developed for a site not previously accessible to the public – a disused company access tunnel with a rather romantic history, albeit a history that relates to a regime of segregation between men and women. The tunnel ran under Bournville Lane from the Cadbury's factory into the Women's Recreation Grounds. The Men's Recreation Grounds are at the far end of this part of the tunnel, so in all likelihood this could have been the site for brief encounters between the two parties. Locked for many years, the tunnel was most recently used for storage. Coley proposed that it should be opened to the public for the duration of the exhibition, with people's movement through the reclaimed space becoming part of the work. He wanted the work 'to deal with the question of meaning in architecture, as used by architects to neutralise or control the masses through style'.

The first element of the project is a reworking of the 'New York Skyline' photograph taken at the 1931 Beaux Arts Ball in Manhattan, where the architects of the Empire State Building, the Chrysler Building and other notable skyscrapers dressed up as their own most famous works. In effect, they were wearing their architectural style and expressing their concerns in relation to the human body, even if this was done in the form of self-parody. To make his work, Coley produced a series of architectural models which could be worn as hats, including a model of the central building in Bournville, the Rest House, which also features in the logo of the Bournville Village Trust. He commissioned a photographer to document five people wearing their hats, or maybe their beliefs, on their heads: 'I think it is crucial that the only "real" building in the collection is the existing Rest House and that the others refer to "what could be".' A text accompanying the photograph suggests that an architectural competition has been run to replace the Rest House with a new building. The people coming across the work, be they locals or just visitors, are implicated in this fictional process; they could allow the place to stay the same or initiate change. That they had willingly entered into a reclaimed architectural site where they were then confronted with the proposition of making a decision about the future nature of their environment was further emphasised by the layout of the tunnel – in order to leave, visitors had to make a choice between two possible exit routes.

From
Gavin Wade, *In the Midst of Things: A Utopian Manual*, August Media, London 2000

Standing in the centre, Ben Simpson adopts a conservational stance, depicting the existing Bournville Rest House built by Harvey and Hicks in 1914. Due for demolition, it is the site for the competition. On the far left, Graham Phillips has declined the invitation to build. Preferring to return to nature, his plan is to simply landscape the site. Susan Harrison proposes a circular meditation space. A polished cast-concrete construction with no window or openings. The faithfulness to the design condemns her to temporary blindness. Simon Henderson's entry is a single-level glass preaching house, illustrating a religious transparency and spiritual openness. Outshining them all, Anne Ferriss has developed a more organic building which is said to stimulate personal growth and enlightenment.

Landmark Portraits

THIS ONGOING, OCCASIONAL SERIES OF PHOTOGRAPHS SHOWS THE ARTIST IN SITES OF HISTORICAL AND/OR POLITICAL RESONANCE, THE IMAGES MAKING THEIR MEANING THROUGH THE ARTIST'S INTERVENTION INTO AND INTERACTION WITH, THE LANDSCAPE IN WHICH HE PLACES HIMSELF.

... / Coley's *Landmark Portraits* make explicit many of the themes with which his practice is intimately involved. Images of an individual inhabiting – and making some kind of a claim to – public space, they engage immediately with the question of what it means for somewhere to exist in the public domain.

Although the photographs take as their starting point the habit of all of us to have our photographs taken in front of famous landmarks in order to mark our visit to a new place, none of the national, cultural and historical landmarks Coley enlists in this series actually appear in it, and only one of them even exists at the time of the image's making. They are all, however, of profound significance for a wide group of people, their importance, and the collective mental space they occupy, out of all proportion to their actual location in the world.

In *Photographing Tate Modern*, Coley turns his back on St Paul's, London's most famous landmark, and the one whose protected sightlines regulate all new building in the capital, to concentrate his camera's attention on the power station that would soon be Tate Modern. Taken before the 'wobbly' bridge linking the two buildings was built, the photograph now seems prophetic of the effect that the new Tate has

had on the cultural geography of London.

In *Reading Burns to the Scott Monument*, Coley stands in Edinburgh's Princes Street Gardens, at the foot of the steps leading to the imposing monument to Sir Walter Scott (1771–1832), the prolific Victorian writer who is the source of much civic pride in the city of Edinburgh. The monument itself now gives definition to one of the city's most famous public gardens, and articulates one particular public face of Edinburgh. Reading the work of Robert Burns (1756–1796) to Scott, Coley brings together two of Scotland's famous sons, the second of whom has no monument dedicated to him. For *Applauding the Millennium Dome*, the artist had himself photographed in Greenwich, London, on the waste ground on which the Dome, the most controversial element of the nation's Millennium celebrations, and, arguably, their biggest failure, was to be built. For *Searching for the Crystal Palace* he visited the site on which Joseph Paxton's immense iron and glass building (destroyed by fire in 1936), was built to stage the Great Exhibition of 1851, a much earlier, and hugely successful tribute to the 'greatness' of Britain. *Waiting on the Scottish Parliament* sees Coley back in Edinburgh, sitting on a bench – that most potent signifier of public space – waiting for the new Scottish parliament building, again a subject of great national controversy, to be built.

The series questions the power that monuments have, and examines the way meaning attaches to buildings over time until they become symbolic of

something often unrelated to their original purpose. In dealing with the ownership of public space, it also questions notions of authorship and art: Coley's ability to take de facto ownership of the Scottish parliament by lounging around on a bench waiting for it to be built, is something that potentially belongs to us all.

Reading Burns to the Scott Monument, Edinburgh 1999

Waiting on the Scottish Parliament, Edinburgh 1999

Searching for the Crystal Palace, London 1999

Applauding the Millennium Dome, London 1999

Fourteen Churches of Münster

FOURTEEN CHURCHES OF MÜNSTER IS A VIDEO TAKEN FROM A HELICOPTER FLYING A CIRCULAR ROUTE OVER FOURTEEN CHURCHES IN THE GERMAN CITY OF MÜNSTER. THE VIDEO IS SHOWN ON A MONITOR, TOGETHER WITH A PLAN OF THE HELICOPTER'S FLIGHT PATH.

... / The plan drawing depicts the flight path taken by a helicopter over the city of Münster in December 1999, the route prescribed by Nathan Coley as the starting point for his work *Fourteen Churches of Münster*. Taking in the whole of central Münster, the route moves from one church to another, circling each one approached.

The video footage made during the short flight presents a bird's eye view of the city and of its religious buildings in particular. The helicopter's speed of movement inevitably transforms the city into an abstract assemblage of lines, shapes and colours, slowing only to examine in detail the churches it seeks. Allowing an unfamiliar perspective on the city, the work articulates the relationship between plan and volume, between earth and heaven.

Even in our secular age, the city cathedral is likely to feature on a postcard, to be the trademark, landmark structure of any city. The religious necessity may have dissipated, but our adoration of the power, the ambition, the scale of these constructed spaces endures. They are emblematic of the civilised and civilising society that created and now maintains them. These buildings can be read as the constructed manifestations of human faith, buildings to which the notion of sacrifice pertains as

much, if not more, than that of architecture.

It is not the church we want, but the sacrifice; not the emotion of admiration, but the act of adoration: not the gift, but the giving. JOHN RUSKIN, *THE SEVEN LAMPS OF ARCHITECTURE*, 1848

The action of Coley's video is not, however, only an exercise in facilitating an abnormal view of the built environment. In the particular context of Münster, it also recalls the perspective of Allied bomber pilots at the end of the Second World War. The intense aerial bombing inflicted on Münster was intended specifically to destroy morale, not strategic military installations. In the Münster Stadtmuseum, there is a transcript from a bomber pilot that reads: 'The field order was coming in on the teletype and we learned that our target was to be the front steps of Münster cathedral'. The instruction was targeting the building as both the physical and spiritual heart of the city. Seen as targets from above, such buildings would have to be stripped of their emotive associations.

Such recognition of the social significance of religious buildings in particular accrues from both their architectural merit and their function as places of communal gathering. The still exceptional scale and degree of ornamentation visible in the churches in Coley's video is testament to the buildings' requirement to express the extent of their congregations' devotion. Like most ecclesiastical architecture, they are exemplary of what John Ruskin called true

architecture which he wrote, must dignify and ennoble public life. 'It must not adulterate the nature of the material it uses. It must be vital, powerful and capable of perpetuating as living history the society which produced it'. (ibid.)

As objects, the particular buildings which are the focus of Coley's work tend skywards, their steeples, towers, pinnacles and roof reaching up to the heavens. From the vantage point of the helicopter, we are given a sense of what it feels like to circle, to target, to objectify places of faith, to intercede between earth and sky, to counter the steeple's spiritual aspiration. But it also allows us rare access to the phenomenal decorative detail rendered to articulate the act of adoration.

Recreating the detached view of the bomber pilots, Coley's video allows us to see these significant buildings as objects. The unfamiliar aerial view – what could be supposed as God's view – exposes the form of the built environment, recalling the plan from which it originates. It reveals the abstract forms imposed on the environment, the footprint of buildings, their hold on the ground. Unlike the plan that lies beneath the flight plan, with its transparent order and layering, ironic rendering of function, the video shows the building as object, distinct from the building as function, as space, as surface, as threshold.

From
Katrina M. Brown,
Fourteen Churches of Münster,
Westfälischer Kunstverein,
Münster 2000

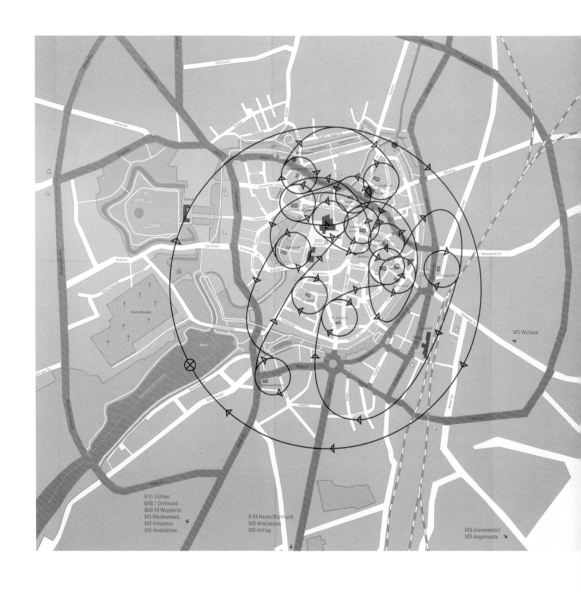

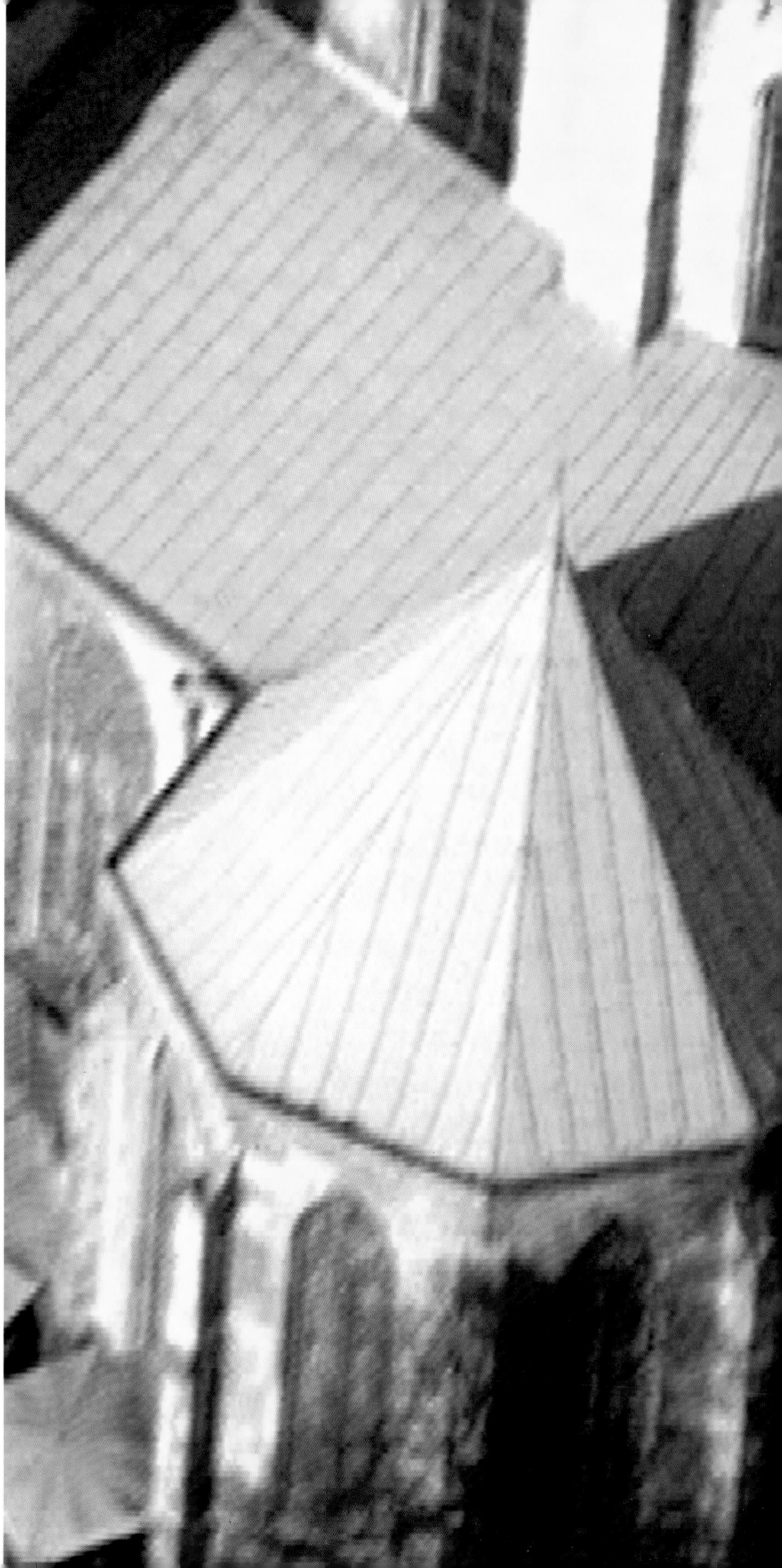

International Style

THIS WORK CONSISTS OF
INTERVIEWS FILMED AT THE
ARCHITECTURAL ASSOCIATION IN
LONDON, WHOSE STUDENTS THE
ARTIST DESCRIBES AS 'THE FUTURE
BUILDERS OF THE WORLD'. THE
INTERVIEWS ARE SHOWN ON TWO
SCREENS FACING ONE ANOTHER,
WITH THE QUESTIONS EDITED OUT.
THE AUDIENCE SEES AND HEARS
ONLY THE STUDENTS RESPONDING
TO UNKNOWN QUESTIONS OF
NATIONALITY, IDENTITY AND BELIEF,
SEEMINGLY TALKING TO ONE
ANOTHER RATHER THAN THE ARTIST.

I AM BELGIAN, AS BELGIAN AS BELGIAN CAN BE. EVERYONE IN THE FAMILY IS BELGIAN; I
MEAN EVERYONE THAT I ORIGINATE FROM. ALTHOUGH IN MY PARENTS' GENERATION PEOPLE
STARTED MARRYING PEOPLE FROM OTHER NATIONALITIES AND IN MY GENERATION PEOPLE STARTED
TO TRAVEL – BUT BEFORE, EVERYONE IS FLEMISH.

I SUPPOSE I SHOULD SAY I'M EUROPEAN, BECAUSE IN TERMS OF NATIONALITY OFFICIALLY I'M
IRISH, BUT BEING THAT MY MOTHER'S SPANISH, MY FATHER'S SPANISH, AND HAVING LIVED IN
DIFFERENT PLACES IN EUROPE I'D ONLY CONSIDER MYSELF NOT HAVING A NATIONALITY.

The Lamp of Sacrifice, 161 Places of Worship, Birmingham 2000

THIS PROJECT, PART OF THE GROUP EXHIBITION *AS IT IS* AT IKON GALLERY IN BIRMINGHAM IN 2000, INVOLVED COLEY MAKING FOUR FOOT HIGH CARDBOARD MODELS OF EVERY PLACE OF WORSHIP LISTED IN THE CITY'S YELLOW PAGES. THE ARTIST MADE THE MODELS IN THE SPACE OF THE GALLERY THROUGHOUT THE DURATION OF THE EXHIBITION.

... / Coley's work has taken a range of forms. from the loaded proposition of an urban sanctuary in Edinburgh to the visual potency of aerial video footage over the churches of Münster in Germany. Each project has been characterised by his considered approach to context. Whilst allowing for the development of ideas around secular and spiritual investment in the physical environment, Coley's commitment to research grounds his responses in the experience of those locations. For *as it is*, Coley pushes the physical and conceptual limits of his practice, to find the means of extending the work and his understanding of it.

During the forty-six days of the exhibition, Coley is constructing cardboard models of every place of worship listed in the Central Birmingham issue of the Yellow Pages. There are 161. Found between Pizza Delivery and Planning, the alphabetical list of Places of Worship acts as a leveller of denominations and renders religion a service like any other. Coley works from digital photographs, which roughly indicate the buildings in three dimensions.They range from a mosque in a terraced house in Kings Heath to a Buddhist temple by the Edgbaston Reservoir.

To Coley, however, they are decontextualised, digital facsimiles, though collectively they form a vision of the city's spiritual aspirations.

Coley's make-shift studio for this laborious process is located in Ikon's second floor galleries, at once an integral part of the group exhibition, yet clearly an autonomous work-in-progress. As models of buildings imbued with meaning, the objects may attract attention, provoking a range of responses and discussion. Yet for Coley it is the process of production (making four models per day for seven weeks) which aligns the work with John Ruskin's belief that, *'It is not the church we want, but the sacrifice; not the emotion of admiration, but the act of adoration: not the gift, but the giving'* (John Ruskin, *The Seven Lamps of Architecture*, 1848). Hence the work's title.

Crucially, what distinguishes Coley's personal involvement in this process of sacrifice from a durational spectacle is the viewer's response to the act itself. In the gallery Coley as 'artist' or 'craftsman' recedes, overshadowed by the identities of the places of worship themselves, their locations marked like targets on the city map. Coley's process of production compresses the construction of these buildings. They become merely signs of the built environment, emptied of their significance and meaning.

From
Claire Doherty, *as it is*, Ikon Gallery, Birmingham 2000

Homes for Heroes
~~Hurt~~ Burn me Daddy

THESE TWO WORKS ARE BOTH MODELS OF BUILDINGS WHICH HAVE FALLEN INTO DISUSE, REMADE BY THE ARTIST AND PRESENTED AS SCULPTURE. ONE IS A DERELICT WAREHOUSE TO WHICH THE ARTIST HAS ADDED THE RESONANT INSCRIPTION 'HOMES FOR HEROES'. THE OTHER IS A MUCH SMALLER, ARCHITECTURALLY IMPOVERISHED BUILDING, ITS INSCRIPTION A FAITHFUL RENDERING OF GRAFFITI SCRAWLED ON IT.

... / **BK** Tell me more about the inscription HOMES FOR HEROES. Where does it come from? Would you mind if one reads it as a reference to Late Modernity, i.e. as a slightly run-down sanatorium for utopian ideals?

NC 'Homes fit for Heroes' was a phrase used by the British Prime Minister Lloyd George during the First World War as a promise to soldiers fighting in the trenches of the Somme. In return for having to go through the horrors of war, the nation would build high-quality houses for them to come back to. I have incorporated the phrase in this work because without that specific reference, place and time, it has many additional readings and can be beautifully misunderstood.

BK What about the inscription '~~HURT~~, BURN ME DADDY' which appears as graffiti on one of the buildings that served as a reference for your work? It points to an individual, rather than a collective frame of mind.

NC At first the text seems to be horrific, making you wonder about the state of mind of the author. It's a terrible thing to write, and a terrible thing to be left on the wall of a building. I think I first saw it two years ago, and it is still there. What happened here? The writing then the rewriting of the text seem to be so angry, so crazed. A friend said it might be a junkie quote, a crack-cocaine thing. So the implication is that this building now has a very specific use, one which has come about through disuse and neglect.

BK Could both images then be said to refer to the coming of age – the point at which, or just after which, decay kicks in – of a civic community as we know it? And how far do they outline a possible point of departure, a chance to change the way of things?

NC There are two things going on here. One is the issue of the relationship between the built environments and politics, while the other is much more to do with our individual use of architecture. It is the interplay between these two that I am interested in. Of course, governmental housing strategies affect people, and the use of certain areas and buildings for drug abuse eventually has to be dealt with in the political arena.

BK As in these new pieces, your recent work mainly deals with architecture, and the relation between scale model, sculpture and installation. Yet your practice is not to be aligned with the all-pervading discourse on urbanism, architectural engineering and design that finally seems to have taken over the art world.

NC I'm really happy to utilise the history and language of architecture and design, but I am much more interested in how values and beliefs are articulated in the urban environment. As for the ever-present discussion about the blurring of boundaries between these disciplines, I feel very clear about where I stand. I am a specialist, not a pluralist. My position is unequivocal, I am an artist. It is only from such a specific vantage point using information from other areas, that I am able to make the work I wish to make.

From
'A Republican Heaven on Earth', interview between Nathan Coley and Boris Kremer, *Audit*, Casino Luxembourg, Luxemburg 2001

What do you think happens to you when you die?

IN THIS PROJECT, MEMBERS OF
THE MÜNSTER KUNSTVEREIN WERE
ASKED THE SAME QUESTIONS AS
THE ARCHITECTURE STUDENTS IN
INTERNATIONAL STYLE. UNLIKE THE
STUDENTS, WHO CAME FROM ALL
OVER THE WORLD AND
REPRESENTED A HUGE RANGE OF
RELIGIONS AND BELIEFS, THE
INDIVIDUALS QUESTIONED HERE
WERE ALL FROM MÜNSTER, ALL
LIVED IN MÜNSTER, AND HAD ALL
BEEN RAISED IN THE CATHOLIC
FAITH. THE TEXTS BELOW ARE
TRANSLATED FROM GERMAN.

IN MY DYING I SHALL LEAVE MYSELF TO THE ONE THAT CREATED AND WANTED ME IN THIS WORLD,
AND I AM SURE THAT I WILL THEN REACH THE LIFE OF RESURRECTION, IN THE GRACE OF GOD.
I AM NOT QUITE SURE HOW THIS WILL BE. PERHAPS COMPLETELY DIFFERENT FROM HOW I IMAGINE
IT. EVEN WHETHER IT WILL HAPPEN, NO ONE KNOWS FOR CERTAIN.

I BELIEVE THAT MY BODY AND MY SOUL WILL DIE AND NO LONGER EXIST, AND NOTHING WILL
FOLLOW, BUT THAT THE PEOPLE WHO KNEW ME WILL REMEMBER ME, AND THAT I WILL LIVE ON
IN THEIR HEADS.

The Land Marked

THE LAND MARKED IS A LARGE VIDEO PROJECTION SHOWN TOGETHER WITH A WALL DRAWING. THE VIDEO IS AN ANIMATION OF ARCHIVE PHOTOGRAPHS DOCUMENTING THE DEMOLITION OF TWO CHIMNEYS NEAR THE FAMOUS BELÉM TOWER IN LISBON. THE WALL DRAWING MARKS THE RELATIVE POSITIONS OF THE TOWER, THE LAND AND THE SEA.

... / *The Land Marked* is inspired by the Belém Tower, one of Lisbon's most emblematic monuments. The work begins by showing the tower in a context that no longer exists: the monument appears flanked by two industrial chimneys. This image, clearly old, becomes, transferred to video, animated and somehow real. The next image shows the two chimneys being blown up, with appropriate sound – boom, boom! – leaving the Tower in the centre, liberated from its industrial framework. In the subsequent sequence of images, the event is inverted so that it is the Belém Tower that implodes and vanishes, leaving the chimneys gazing at the empty centre of the image. Finally we see the Tower and its surroundings as they are today. This is all repeated on a loop.

Not everything in *The Land Marked* is fiction: the industrial chimneys really did exist, and their demolition was recorded in black and white images taken by an anonymous photographer and retrieved from the City Photographic Archives by the artist. The title of the work alludes to the historical importance of the Belém Tower as a Lisbon landmark, but it also has a more general meaning: that of marked earth or territory. This moves the debate on from one concerning a physical, tangible entity, made in monumental stone and a familiar point of reference in the city's geography, to one concerned with more abstract and symbolic issues.

Coley not only refreshes our memory of the context in which one of Lisbon's major monuments exists as part of our national and tourist landscape, but also makes us aware that this monument has not existed for ever, that many other monuments have been destroyed, and that some were conceived but never built. The work subtly questions the European doctrine of heritage and preservation. Or rather, the work refuses to take that doctrine as a given, but instead questions it as an ideology which results from a series of ideals that have been set in stone over the centuries.

Unlike other cultures, Europe tends to view its architecture as eternal, but it is obvious that it is not, and that fact entails a constant choice between what is to be maintained and what may be destroyed. The issue of functionality that is so dear to artistic discourse must then be readdressed. If a work of art distinguishes itself from non-art objects by its lack of functionality, and is created without any other function than its pure creation, then what are we to make of a building that has long ceased to be functional, which no longer serves the objective of national defence for which it was originally created? A politician or proud citizen might answer this question simply by citing its symbolic, historical and artistic importance. And these are the criteria that undoubtedly led to the decision to remove the factory, which was, at the time, utilitarian and functional.

It is the deconstruction of these different levels of meaning that interests Coley. The artist uses virtual technology not to create supposed scenarios of the future, but rather to revisit or confuse scenarios of the past, and it is clear that what concerns him is not architecture, buildings or monuments, but the discourse that surrounds them; the social, political, ideological and aesthetic impact they provoke. Coley's work consistently aims to show how urban space and what takes place within it can be a point of departure from which to question our own perceptions and the commonplaces on which our particular world-views are constructed. And the expression 'commonplaces' has two meanings here: on the one hand, it refers to commonly shared urban spaces; on the other, it alludes to common sense, that basic level of received knowledge.

It is not only perception, but also representation and its mechanisms that are questioned by this work. By combining original photographs with other, manipulated and virtual images, Coley works on that very thin line between reality and fiction, the representation of reality and simulacrum.

From
Isabel Carlos, 'Ceci n'est pas un ...', *From Work To Text: Dialogues on Practice and Criticism in Contemporary Art*, Fundação Centro Cultural de Belém, Lisbon 2002

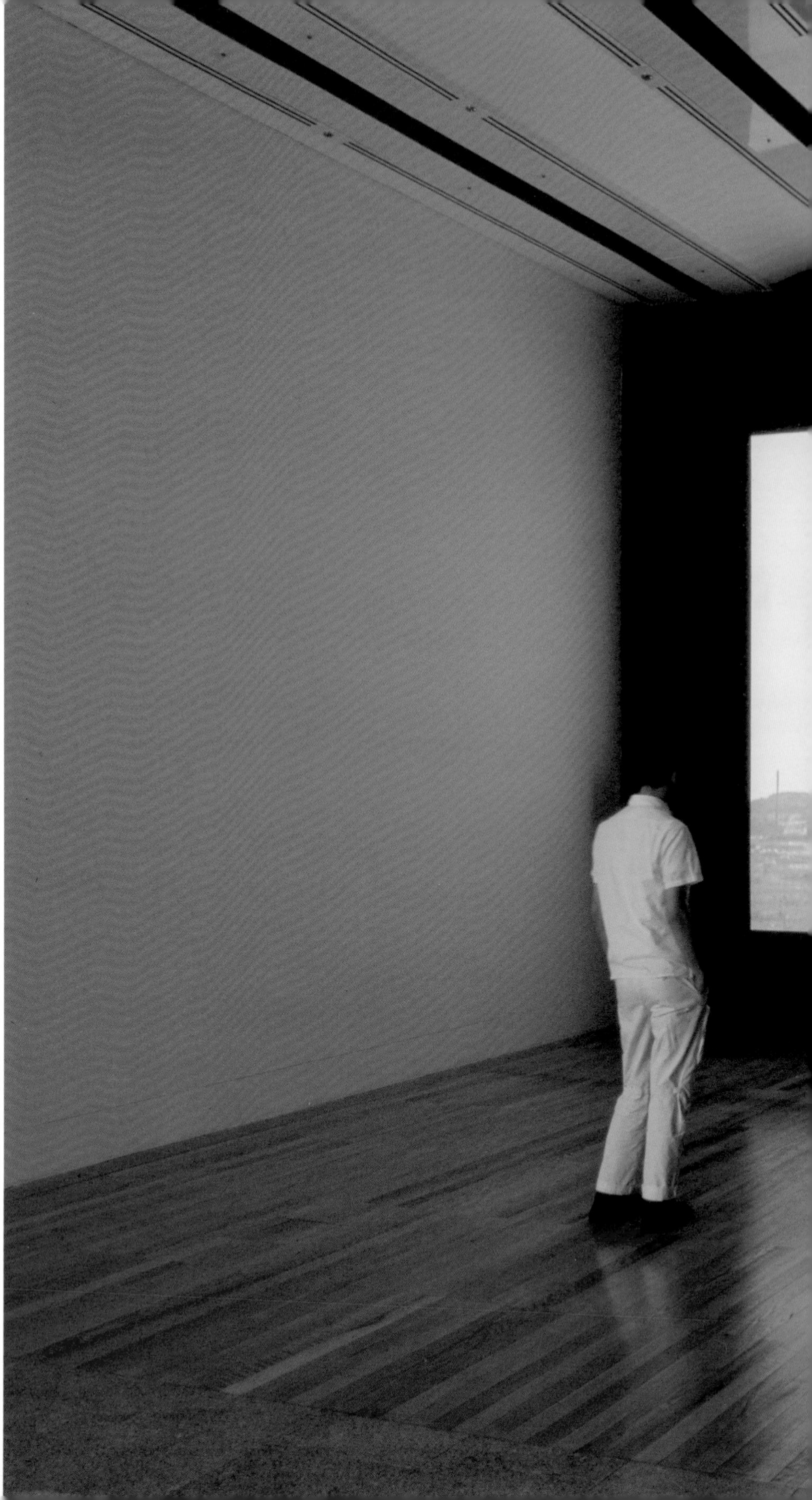

The Italian Tower

THE ITALIAN TOWER WAS A
TEMPORARY WORK OF PUBLIC
SCULPTURE, CONSTRUCTED FROM
PLYWOOD AND TERRACOTTA TILES
IN THE PUBLIC CAR PARK OUTSIDE
THE VISITORS' CENTRE OF THE
KIELDER RESERVOIR IN
NORTHUMBERLAND IN 2001. IT WAS
THEN MOVED AND SITED IN THE
RESERVOIR FOR THE DURATION OF
THE SUMMER.

... / A constructed piece of fiction,
The Italian Tower was an obviously
artificial element in a less-
obviously artificial environment.
The Kielder Reservoir is a man-
made lake, set in a managed
forest. People visit the Reservoir
as an environmental attraction;
visitors can take boat tours and
even fish. The flooding of the
valley to create the Reservoir took
place within living memory,
however, and there are those who
remember both the valley and the
village which was set in it and
which now lies submerged
beneath the lake. Coley made
The Italian Tower not as a remnant
of the lost village (the foreignness
of its architecture instantly
precluded that possibility) but
rather as an encouragement to
visitors to the Reservoir to rethink
their ideas of what is 'natural'
in the natural environment, and
what is not.

Coley's tower was part of a
programme of temporary and
permanent artworks sited in the
landscape at Kielder, and featured
in the commentary to the summer
boat tour:

*Coming up on our left is 'The
Italian Tower' by Nathan Coley,
one of our artworks here at
Kielder. It was initially fabricated in
the car park at Leaplish, prior to
being transported across the water*

*and reconstructed as we see it
here. Made from timber, plywood
and ceramic tiles, it stands five
and a half metres above the water,
a landmark for fishermen and bird
life alike.*

The Black Maria

INVITED TO PARTICIPATE IN *SCAPE: ART AND INDUSTRY URBAN ARTS BIENNALE* 2002 IN CHRISTCHURCH, NEW ZEALAND, THE ARTIST BUILT A SCULPTURE REMINISCENT OF A STAGE SET FOR A SILENT WESTERN ON THE ROOF OF ONE OF THE CITY'S ART GALLERIES.

... / Works sited within 'a particular place ... speak in a symbolic tongue about the meaning or use of that place', and *The Black Maria*'s short-lived presence here cast a long dark shadow indeed. In preparation for this project, the artist Nathan Coley with curator Juliana Engberg and project manager Geraldine Barlow took the tram around town, taking in the views afforded them of the city. The neo-Gothic frames of Mountfort's architecture, the saloon-style 'Vic 'n' Whale' and the Colonial Spanish chic of new Regent's Street, led them to conclude that Christchurch is a 'city of nostalgic façades ... a frontier town'.

Accepting for a moment that geographically and conceptually Christchurch may have been a new frontier for the Scottish artist 'way down South', it must be remembered that we live in an age when the foundational assumptions of any centre/periphery model are up for re-evaluation and potential re-configuration, most obviously on those so-called 'margins'. As a consequence of this, any gesture towards 'frontier living' necessarily provides an opportunity to unmask and interrogate some of the more complex issues that exist below the surface of those cultural constructions with which we surround ourselves, and to which we have grown accustomed.

History can be seen as a social narrative perpetually constructed and re-constructed, and *The Black Maria*'s presence served forcefully to punctuate the mechanisms of that process through its disruption of the full colour complexity of our lived reality with its monochromatic and anachronistic presence. *The Black Maria* is a prop that also functions as a proposition, raising questions about the role and ambivalence of mimicry, and the story of 'how the West was really won'. It is precisely the work's dramatic narrative potential that makes Coley's gesture so unnerving. This project was the result of an invitation to participate in *Scape: Art and Industry Urban Arts Biennale* 2002 in Christchurch, New Zealand. A sculpture which resembles a stage set for a silent Western was placed on top of the building which houses The Physics Room, one of the town's art galleries. Like its namesake, the first ever film studio, the sculpture rotated 360° to follow the sun. In this instance, The Physics Room can be seen to have both logistically, with Art and Industry, and physically, supported Coley's practice, as the pedestal for his sculptural form looms large, drawing attention to the building itself and the possibilities enabled through contemporary forms of communication. The work itself can also be seen to form part of an expanding network dedicated to the politics of site-specificity and the art of cross-reference.

Avant-garde gestures, such as those fostered by the biennial, can be seen to have 'two audiences, one which was there and one – most of us – which wasn't', and Coley's related installation within the gallery space, *Places Where Something has Happened* plays with this idea, as well as again raising issues about the nature and politics of representation. *The Black Maria* was a silent, ramshackle construction that spoke volumes about the nature and character of our times and through both of his installations Coley compelled us to look beyond the familiar and accepted representations of our culture, to the complex scaffolding and the unstable foundations that we choose to hide beneath those façades.

From
Kate Montgomery, *The Physics Room Annual*, The Physics Room, Christchurch 2002

Ruskin's Road

THIS PROJECT INVOLVED THE ARTIST
STRETCHING A HUGE TARPAULIN
ACROSS A BUILDING SITE IN
LEIDSCHE RIJN, A NEW SUPERCITY
BEING BUILT OUTSIDE UTRECHT IN
HOLLAND. A COMBINATION OF
POLITICAL EXPEDIENCY AND
ENLIGHTED IF POSSIBLY DOOMED
UTOPIANISM, THE NEW CITY WILL
SEE THE VERY BEST ARCHITECTS
ATTEMPT TO BUILD 30,000 LOW-
COST HOUSES IN 15 YEARS.

The great thinker, writer and artist John Ruskin was famous for his meditations on the difference between 'building' and 'architecture' – the former having purely function and the latter meaning. During his time ching at Oxford University he undertook a project with his students to build a road. This as he said was "to teach the students the dignity of labour". It has been recorded that one of the students that collaborated on this journey was a young Oscar Wilde The road itself was unremarkable, but the Process involved in making it truly astonishing.

I Don't Have Another Land

THIS WORK IS AN EXACT, HAND-CRAFTED REPLICA OF THE MARKS & SPENCER'S BUILDING IN MANCHESTER, DEMOLISHED DUE TO THE DAMAGE CAUSED BY AN IRA BOMB IN 1996. PLACED DIRECTLY ON THE FLOOR OF THE GALLERY, DENSELY BLACK AND SOMEWHAT FORBIDDING, IT IS A WORK OF MONUMENTAL SCULPTURE, A TESTAMENT TO SOMETHING, ONCE INTENSELY FAMILIAR TO THE PEOPLE OF MANCHESTER, MADE STRANGE THROUGH LOSS.

... / Nathan Coley's work develops out of an intense scrutiny of a specific building or situation. During the past year he has made a number of sculptures based on buildings which have endured a dramatic change in function or which embody a violent clash of interests – respectable home to squat, garage to drugs den. Dollhouse in scale, these subversive objects playfully defy categorisation. Are they sculptures or architectural models? Are they monuments to architectural development or memorials to loss – symbols of reversed fortunes? I Don't Have Another Land is the newest work in this vein, continuing Coley's interest in oppositional change within the context of Manchester. The work is based on the old Marks & Spencer's building destroyed as a result of the IRA bomb damage. In researching and re-presenting this lost building, Coley gives new consideration to a structure erased from the urban memory by the rush of new plans. To reinforce the significance of the building, this scaled-down version sports a blackened sheen and is accompanied by a phrase taken from an anonymous folk song.

The result is a tense and mischievously evasive object, one that invites us to interpret its function, but ultimately dodges a single analysis.

From
Natalie Rudd, *Fabrications: New Art & Urban Memory in Manchester,* Manchester University Press, Manchester 2002

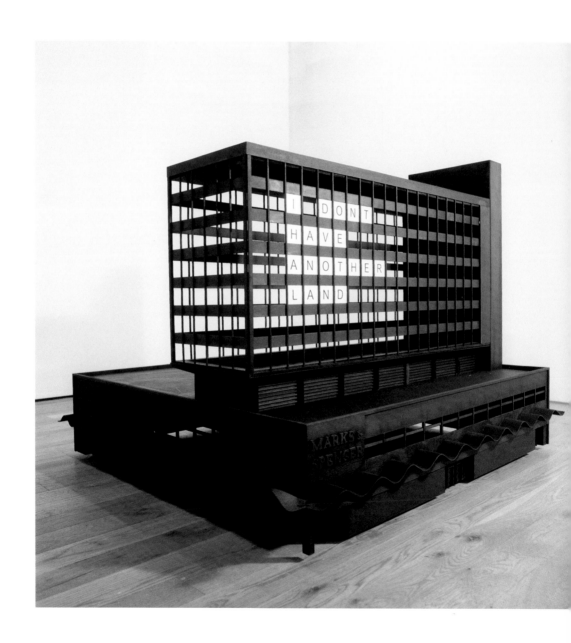

Show Home

SHOW HOME WAS A TEMPORARY PUBLIC ARTWORK IN WHICH THE ARTIST FABRICATED TWO SIDES OF A SMALL COTTAGE, WHICH WAS INSTALLED IN THREE DIFFERENT LOCATIONS ON THREE CONSECUTIVE DAYS IN NORTH SHIELDS, TYNE AND WEAR. INTRINSIC TO THE PROJECT WAS AN EXTENSIVE MARKETING CAMPAIGN COMPLETE WITH LIFESTYLE BROCHURE, WEBSITE, FLAGS AND SIGNBOARDS, DESIGNED TO MIMIC THE SALES TECHNIQUES OF HOUSING DEVELOPERS.

... / Nathan Coley's temporary public art project, Show Home, 2003, takes the form of an unexpected intervention in the urban landscape that questions perceptions of ideal space and the manipulation of lifestyle aspirations. The Show Home is a life-sized, two bedroom house. The architecture is simple and symmetrical – with its white walls and slate roof it is every bit the 'rural retreat' dreamed of by the urban dweller. A closer investigation however reveals that Show Home is nothing more than a stage set. What initially appears to be a typical cottage is actually only a two-sided structure with its back wall missing, a sculpture that feigns the idea of a 'home'.

Curated by Locus+, Show Home was commissioned by North Tyneside Council and was displayed briefly in three different locations in the town of North Shields. This area of the North East of England is known historically for its role in the British fishing industry, a sector now in decline. Consequently North Shields is being rapidly developed as a commuter town, to serve the metropolitan centres of Newcastle upon Tyne and Gateshead, and is often marketed as an ideal location in which to bring up a young family. Isolated and distinctly different from the surrounding architectural environment, Show Home was literally constructed on the last remaining bits of land in the marina area of the town.

Using the language of estate agents and property developers, Coley devised a media campaign to promote Show Home. To convince the viewer-consumer, the prototype cottage was presented on site boards and appeared in newspaper advertisements while the artist gave interviews on television and radio.

Coley states that the sculpture's lack of a back wall, 'pushes the work away from being read as architecture and moves it closer to being sculpture and clearly artifice'. Show Home reveals itself as a work that proposes a different approach to public art. The artist's intention is to create a platform for debate, to question the continuous development of the environment and to discuss art's capacity to intervene in public space.

During its siting around North Shields, Show Home attracted a wide range of people with positive reactions to the development, many of whom even expressed an interest in buying it until they realised that this 'simple traditional house', the 'home they were looking for' according to the brochure, was actually a fake. Show Home seems to offer the opportunity to settle in a dream home and experience an ideal lifestyle, but the illusion is short-lived and in any case, just as quickly as it appears, the house moves on. The theatrical illusion to naturalism in the removal of the back wall simply reminds us that our fantasies are thin: we might be able to gaze into the simulation of an idealised lifestyle but its promise is false.

From
Irini-Mirena Papadimitriou and Lisa Bosse, 'Nathan Coley', Tales of the City, Arte Fiera, Bologna 2004

Lockerbie

LOCKERBIE IS THE RESULT OF THE ARTIST'S PROJECT TO BE UNOFFICIAL ARTIST-IN-RESIDENCE AT KAMP VAN ZEIST IN THE NETHERLANDS, THE SCOTTISH COURT ESTABLISHED IN 2000 IN ORDER TO TRY THE TWO LIBYAN FORMER INTELLIGENCE AGENTS CHARGED WITH THE BOMBING OF FLIGHT PAN AM 103 OVER LOCKERBIE IN 1988. THE WORK INCLUDES A REPLICA OF THE WITNESS BOX USED DURING THE TRIAL, DISPLAYED TOGETHER WITH DRAWINGS OF EVIDENCE PRESENTED TO THE COURT AND A VIDEO. THE ORIGINAL WITNESS BOX IS NOW, THANKS TO THE ARTIST'S INTERVENTION, PART OF THE WEAPONS AND FIREARMS COLLECTION OF THE IMPERIAL WAR MUSEUM IN LONDON.

... / In 2000, the artist Nathan Coley […] applied to be admitted to the Lockerbie trial. The authorities were baffled by his interest in being there with no concrete purpose other than to witness the proceedings as an independent observer. He was accepted, not as an artist but as a journalist, since this was the only category in which they could place him. He was in any case intrigued by the idea that a building could itself inscribe and impose on visitors submission to authority. But was Coley's enforced false identification as a journalist denying that press pass to a bona fide journalist who might have had other questions to ask and other stories to tell? Funded by a grant from the 'Year of the Artist' scheme in Scotland, what were his responsibilities, and to whom? This kind of conceptual conundrum was exactly what drew him to the trial in the first place. It was being held

in a Scottish court, in a site legally designated as Scotland, but geographically in the Netherlands. The staff included Dutch workers, who would wake up in Holland and cycle a mile down the road to this place that had become Scotland. There were Scottish workers, who were working abroad, in Scotland. Equipped with his press pack, which included digitised images of the evidence, Coley sat watching the trial, wondering right up to his final days what exactly he was doing there. Staring at the witness box, he realised that his interest in the trial was contained in the object he was looking at. A constructed space charged with revealing the 'truth', the witness box was a physical symbol of the ideas of truth and conviction that so intrigued him. So much so, that he has collaborated with the Imperial War Museum in London to obtain permission for it to enter their collection.

Coley had an exact replica of the witness box made […]. Reflecting on the trial, he says, 'As an artist, I'm not interested in justice, I'm not necessarily all that interested in revenge, and I'm actually not that interested in the truth either. I'm much more interested in taking on the role of the artist and lying, working with ideas of doubt and uncertainty. I think that's a valuable role for us to take. There are other people who can deal with the truth'. His interest as an artist is in questioning the ways in which philosophical values and beliefs become inscribed in the infrastructure of social and political systems. The ostensible purpose of the Lockerbie trial was to establish whether the accused men had planted the bomb. But at

a deeper level it symbolised and enacted a confrontation between Christian America and Islamic Libya. At the centre of the trial was the witness box – a conceptual device used to elicit truth. Yet it invites projections of truth, both in the courtroom and in the exhibition space where Coley re-presents it. In both situations, the truth will be subjectively constructed. How are we to look at Coley's drawings of the 'evidence', which is made up of ordinary objects and ordinary faces made ominous by the context? Evidence of what exactly? Coley's act of infiltration is an act of scrutiny which peels back the veneer of certainty.

From
Judith Nesbitt, 'On Being Sane in Insane Places', *Days Like These*, Tate Britain, London 2003 © Tate Trustees

Yorkie Clothing

YORKIE CLOTHING INDUSTRY Ltd.

12 New Lane in Villambrosa Str.,
Hamrun   Tel: 623431

Ref
~~Invoice~~ № 18345

Date 18·11·88

To Messrs Gauci

	Delivery Note	@	£m	cm
20	pairs of trs ord 1705 checked Pactory Mat with ept band			
98	pairs of trs ORD 1705 Pact Mat with ept band			
118	TOTAL			

Tony Gau

811363

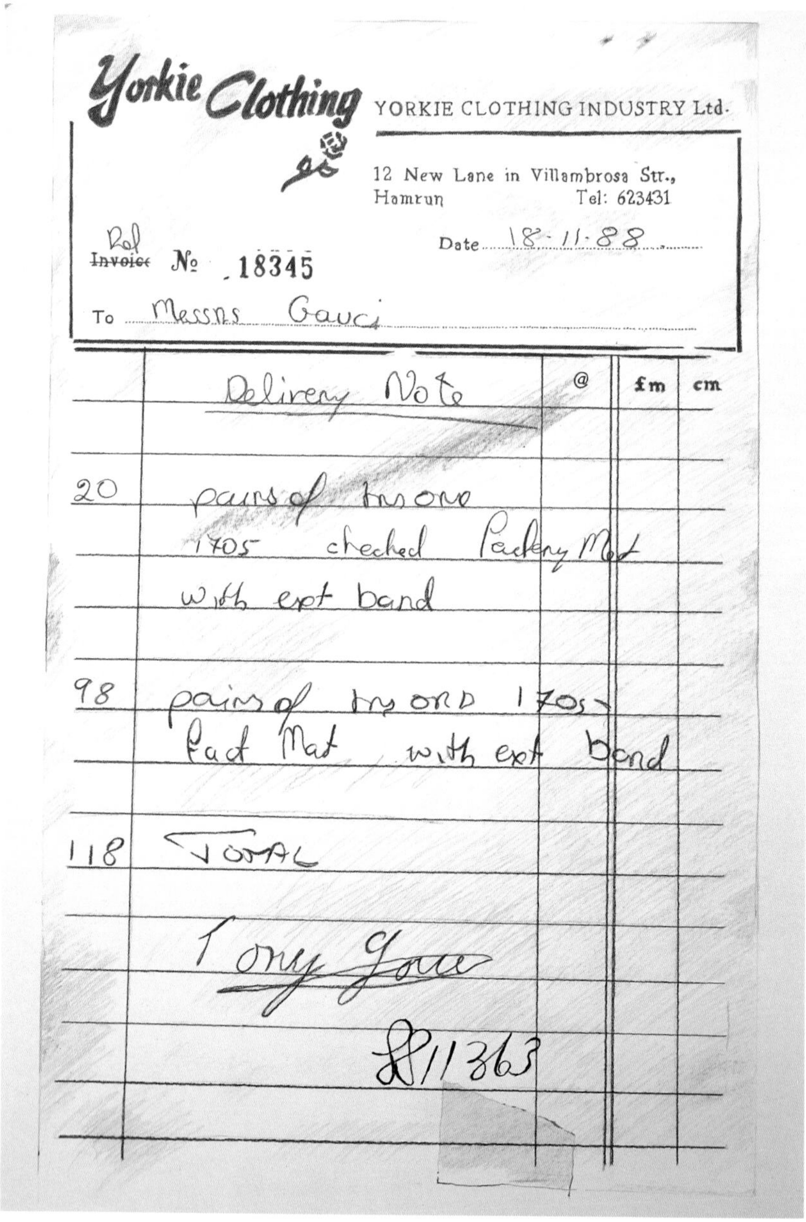

Black Tent

BLACK TENT WAS COMMISSIONED FOR PORTSMOUTH CATHEDRAL. COLEY'S RESPONSE TO THE COMMISSION WAS A PIECE OF FLEXIBLE ARCHITECTURE, A STRONGLY GEOMETRIC ABSTRACT TENT WHICH TOOK UP VARIOUS POSITIONS AROUND THE CATHEDRAL OVER A PERIOD OF SIX WEEKS, OBSCURING SOME SPACES AND REVEALING OTHERS, HINDERING SOME OF THE NORMAL OPERATIONS OF THE CHURCH WHILE OPENING UP POSSIBILITIES FOR NEW WAYS OF BEHAVING WITHIN IT.

... / How do you go about reading a black tent? Like a church, Black Tent contains many specific ideas and also approaches the universal. Unlike a church, and although taking the form of architecture, Black Tent is an artwork, or to be more precise, a sculpture. Black Tent contains elements of symbolism not found within the church's vocabulary and adheres, to varying degrees, to a set of underlying beliefs. The sculpture is not governed by any particular rules or guidelines apart from gravity and other physical laws.

[...] Black Tent consists of ten square panels, each 8ft x 8ft. Each panel is divided into four vertical columns by three slim white lines. Each column can be black, grey or purple. Each column can also be divided so that a transparent, yellow or purple section sits revealing a grid. This insert section is also allowed to spread horizontally across more than one column to make a band, but this is not the dominant form. This abstract geometric system only covers the 'outside' of Black Tent. On the 'inside', all the panels are black, with the transparent inserts

still visible. Each panel is supported by two steel poles with a large circular base. Each panel can be situated at a 90-degree angle or at a 180-degree angle to the previous and one pole is able to become a vertex for a maximum of four panels at 90 degrees to each other in the form of a cross. This system makes it possible for Black Tent to be positioned in a large number of ways and also makes it very difficult to maintain a complete inside and outside of the structure. When connected, the panels form a series of temporary spaces, a temporary building that offers some kind of use, whether as a place of sanctuary or a promotional stage.

[...] Black Tent has many functions. The sculpture seems to propose that it can adapt to different people's needs. Black Tent can be a sanctuary if you want to use it in that way but you could also use the building for storytelling or for architecture workshops or endless types of secular meetings, each event within the work reflective of its structure and precedents. As a 'user' of the artwork you can make the decision yourself. In some ways, it is easy. Allow yourself to impose on the structure your own concerns, needs and desires. Next, imagine a shape that Black Tent could take to best fill your needs. Finally, think of this process as a new beginning and you are fast approaching the moment of discovering meaning. Coley chose the nave of the Cathedral as the site for Black Tent to come in to the world based on the history of the use of the space. In the guide book to the Cathedral it says,

'With no fixed furniture, the nave has the feeling of a gathering space, a market place. In this sense it is rather like the atrium in front of an early Roman Basilica. Here people gathered before worship – it was an enlarged entrance hall. There is a strong feeling in the nave that we are "outside" the main body of the church.' Coley chose the nave as it has exactly this: a public feel to it. It also is the most simple and unarticulated area of the building, has good natural light and can be seen from many points. Its starting point is clear, its use is open. Black Tent was moved to the opposite, east end of the Cathedral along the Christian story from the newest part to the oldest. In St Thomas's Chapel Black Tent partially enclosed the chancel consecrated in 1188 and the pyx (sometimes known as the tabernacle) containing the elements of the sacrament for use in communion. Black Tent became the space in which the most sacred ceremonies of the Cathedral would take place for a two-week period before moving out to other parts of the city to act in entirely different ways. How you use the artwork does not take away from it being art, it is merely an inherent purpose and part of its workings as an abstract artwork.

From
Gavin Wade, 'How to read a black tent, tabernacles and other stories', Black Tent, Art in Sacred Places, London 2003

The Lamp of Sacrifice, 286 Places of Worship, Edinburgh 2004

A DEVELOPMENT OF THE PROJECT MADE IN BIRMINGHAM, THIS WORK CONSISTS OF CARDBOARD MODELS OF EVERY PLACE OF WORSHIP LISTED IN THE 2004 YELLOW PAGES FOR EDINBURGH. INSTEAD OF BEING MADE IN THE GALLERY IN THE PRESENCE OF THE AUDIENCE, HOWEVER, THIS TIME THE SCULPTURES WERE MADE IN THE PRIVACY OF THE ARTIST'S STUDIO AND PRESENTED, FINISHED AND IMMACULATE, FROM THE FIRST DAY OF THE EXHIBITION.

... / As with *The Lamp of Sacrifice, 161 Places of Worship, Birmingham 2000*, this work has its origins in John Ruskin's discussion of the meaning of architecture being embedded in the notion of a sacrifice being involved in its making. The places of worship which serve as the pattern for the artist's models have this kind of meaning – they are the tangible result of a specific desire to create a place and a space for the contemplation of something other than the everyday, and stand for the coming together of a community.

By remaking the buildings, Coley invites us to reconsider them and the congregations who give them meaning. He himself has made few decisions about them. No subjectivity enters into his selection, rather he makes a model of every place of worship that chooses to list itself in the Yellow Pages (in the case of Edinburgh, a vast listing, with the geographical area covered stretching over the Forth Bridge into Fife to the north and down into the Borders on a level with Newcastle upon Tyne to the south). He makes the models out of cardboard, in the colour that cardboard is, and has developed a

system for making them which, though allowing for a surprising level of detail, is schematic, and based primarily on speed.

In opting to revisit the idea of reinvesting a city's places of worship with Ruskinian meaning through the Herculean task of remaking them out of cardboard, the artist has made a significant alteration to his original project. This time, presented as it is in the context of a solo exhibition, the work is made entirely behind the scenes, all trace of performance – of the artist actually making them – kept well out of sight and in the past. The sacrifice is still there, but it is at one remove. This inevitably changes the work. No longer is the artist there to interrogate directly. The models must speak for him.

Immediately, they speak of skill and even beauty, a breathtaking sea of models spilling exuberantly over the floor of the gallery, surrounding the viewer with instance after instance of delight that a building could have been so perfectly captured in cardboard. Secondly, however, they speak of endeavour, and of a personal sacrifice of considerable time and effort. On close inspection, they offer no illusion; all the artist's working pencil marks remain to help the viewer see how each model has been painstakingly constructed from a flat sheet of cardboard scored, folded and glued in response to the dictates of four digital photographs, the artist's only point of reference in the real world of the buildings themselves. Clearly, it is not the models themselves that interest the artist, nor even the individual buildings – none is named or even visibly numbered; there is nothing to help us find St Mary's or

St Giles's Cathedrals, nor any of the city's other religious landmarks in the bewildering mass of cardboard models.

The important thing for the artist – and for the work – is that the models have been made, by hand, over a set and sacrificial period of time, in this case the 15 weeks between the beginning of February 2004 and the opening of the exhibition for which they were commissioned. Making every place of worship listed in a city's Yellow Pages is a way of mapping that city, of understanding it and taking its measure. All of Edinburgh's aspirations and ambitions, looked at from a very particular, if pluralist perspective, are contained in the work. It speaks of social politics and possibility. It offers a definition, right here and right now, of what Edinburgh is.

A SERIES OF PRINTS ACCOMPANIES
*THE LAMP OF SACRIFICE, 286
PLACES OF WORSHIP, EDINBURGH
2004*. THE ARTIST HAS SELECTED TEN
OF THE MODELS MADE FOR THE
INSTALLATION TO BE
PHOTOGRAPHED ALONE, ON A
NEUTRAL GROUND. AS EVER, THE
INDIVIDUAL IDENTITY OF EACH PLACE
OF WORSHIP, PRESENTED FLOATING
IN SPACE LIKE AN UNASSAILABLE
ARCHITECTURAL ARCHETYPE, IS
LESS INTERESTING TO COLEY THAN
THE CHALLENGE THEY
COLLECTIVELY POSE TO HIM AS A
MODEL MAKER. ALTHOUGH EACH IS
SUFFICIENT TO ITSELF, THE SERIES
OF PRINTS WORK TOGETHER TO
BRING THE PROJECT BACK TO
WHERE IT STARTED, THE NAMES OF
THE PLACES OF WORSHIP FORMING
A LIST REMINISCENT OF THE YELLOW
PAGES WITH WHICH THE ARTIST
BEGAN.

PLACES OF WORSHIP

See also: **Religious organisations**

Abbotshall Church,Abbotshall Rd.............. **Kirkcaldy (01592)** 204319
Abundant Life Church,Fairhurst Drive.......... **Hawick (01450)** 374305
Armadale Parish Church,Academy St........ **Armadale (01501)** 732314
Assembly of God Church,
49 Bridge St,Musselburgh,EH21.............. (0131) 665 0303
Baptist Church The,1 Victoria Rd.............. **N Berwick (01620)** 895463
Barclay Church,1 Wrights Houses,EH10.............. (0131) 229 6810
Bellevue Baptist Church,29 Arthur St,EH6.............. (0131) 551 5191
Bellevue Chapel,Rodney St,EH7.............. (0131) 557 9689
Blackhall St. Columba,Queensferry Rd,EH4.............. (0131) 332 4431
Bo'Ness Old Parish Church,Panbrae Rd....... **Bo'Ness (01506)** 822756
Bowmont Street Christian Centre,
52a Bowmont St.............. **Kelso (01573)** 228064
Bristo Baptist Church,
Buckingham Terrace Queensferry Rd,EH4.............. (0131) 332 3682
Broughton St. Mary's Church Centre,
7 East Broughton Place,EH1.............. (0131) 556 4252
Broxburn Parish Church of Scotland,
Parish Church East Main St.............. **Broxburn (01506)** 852825
Bruntsfield Evangelical Church,
70 Leamington Terrace,EH10.............. (0131) 229 0127
Buccleuch & Greyfriars Free Church,
8 West Crosscauseway,EH8.............. (0131) 667 0867
Carrick Knowe Parish Church,
Saughton Road North,EH12.............. (0131) 334 1505
Carrubber's Christian Centre,65 High St,EH1.............. (0131) 556 2626
Catholic Church,
St. Cuthberts High Cross Avenue,Melrose.... **Galashiels (01896)** 752328
St. Mary & David,15 Buccleuch St.............. **Hawick (01450)** 372037
St. Cuthberts Chapel Westfield Rd,Earlston....... **Selkirk (01750)** 21779
Catholic Church of St. John Cantius & St. Nicholas,
West Main St.............. **Broxburn (01506)** 852040
Cellardyke Parish Church,Cellardyke......**Anstruther (01333)** 310810
Charlotte Baptist Chapel,13 South Charlotte St,EH2.... (0131) 225 4812
Christadelphian Church,4 Gayfield Place,EH7.............. (0131) 556 7958
Christian Science First Church,11 Young St,EH2......... (0131) 225 7676
Christian Science Reading Room,
15 Waterloo Place,EH1.............. (0131) 556 1860
Church of Christ,Garden Place, Eliburn.... **Livingston (01506)** 414879
Church of Christ,
Blair Avenue,Glamis Centre,Pitteuchar,KY7.............. 01592 560912
Church of Christ,48a Gilmerton Dykes Drive,EH17........ (0131) 664 5505
Church of Jesus Christ of Latter Day Saints,
St. Leonards Place.............. **Dunfermline (01383)** 733388
Winifred Crescent.............. **Kirkcaldy (01592)** 640041
Church of Jesus Christ of Latter-day Saints The,
Newbattle Rd,Eskbank,EH22.............. (0131) 654 0630
51 Spylaw Rd,EH10.............. (0131) 337 1283
Church of Nazarene The,
26 Headwell Avenue.............. **Dunfermline (01383)** 741007
Church of the Nazarene,5 Rannoch Terrace,EH4.......... (0131) 339 4581
Clemiston Baptist Church,8 Hoseason Gardens,EH4..... (0131) 336 1476
Cluny Parish Church Centre,1 Cluny Drive,EH10.......... (0131) 447 6745
Colinton Parish Church,Dell Rd,EH13.............. (0131) 441 2232
Community Church Edinburgh,
41a South Clerk St,EH8.............. (0131) 466 8660
Congregational Church,
West End,High St.............. **Kirkcaldy (01592)** 268777
Cornerstone Full Gospel Church,
Four Lums Rd,Aberdour.............. **Dalgety Bay (01383)** 825095
Corstorphine Old Parish Church,
High Street Hall,2a High St,Corstorphine,EH12.............. (0131) 334 7864
(0131) 334 1258
Craiglockhart Parish Church,
Craiglockhart Drive North,EH14.............. (0131) 455 8229
Craigmailen United Free Church,
10 Braehead.............. **Bo'Ness (01506)** 823784
Craigsbank Church Of Scotland,Craigsbank,EH12....... (0131) 334 6365
Cramond Kirk,16 Cramond Glebe Rd,EH4.............. (0131) 336 2036
Currie Kirk,156 Lanark Rd West,Currie,EH14.............. (0131) 451 5141
Dalgety Parish Church,Regents Way.... **Dalgety Bay (01383)** 824092
Dalkeith Baptist Church,North Wynd,Dalkeith,EH22.... (0131) 654 2410
Davidson's Mains Parish Church,1 Quality St,EH4....... (0131) 312 6282
Drylaw Parish Church,Groathill Rd North,EH4.............. (0131) 343 6643
Duke St Cong Church,108 Duke St,EH6.............. (0131) 554 9033
Dunbar Parish Church,Queens Rd.............. **Dunbar (01368)** 865440
Dunfermline Abbey,St. Margaret St..... **Dunfermline (01383)** 724586
Dunfermline Congregational Church,
Church Halls Canmore St.............. **Dunfermline (01383)** 721468
East Craigs Church Centre,Bughtlin Market,EH12........ (0131) 339 8336
Ebenezer United Free Church of Scotland,
31 Bangor Rd,EH6.............. (0131) 553 5243
Edinburgh Spiritualist Society,34 Albany St,EH1........ (0131) 556 1749
Elim Pentecostal Church,
Elim Centre Knightsridge West,Livingston,EH54.............. 01506 497012
Elohim the House of Righteousness,
68 Britwell Crescent,EH7.............. (0131) 663 1760
Ettrick Yarrow Parish Church Of Scotland,
Yarrow Manse,Yarros.............. **Yarrow (01750)** 82336
Fairmilehead Parish Church,
Frogston Rd West,EH10.............. (0131) 445 2374
Franciscans Friary The,
120 Niddrie Mains Rd,Craigmillar,EH16.............. (0131) 661 2185
Free Presbyterian Church Of Scotland,
63 Gilmore Place,EH3.............. (0131) 229 0649
Galashiels Baptist Church,Victoria St....... **Galashiels (01896)** 750248
Gillespie Memorial Church Centre,
Gillespie Centre Chapel St.............. **Dunfermline (01383)** 621253
Gilmerton Church of Scotland,Ravenscroft St,EH17.... (0131) 664 7538
Glenrothes Baptist Church,
8 Church St.............. **Glenrothes (01592)** 754373
Glenrothes Christ's Kirk,
Pitcoudie Avenue.............. **Glenrothes (01592)** 745938
Gorgie Parish Church,190 Gorgie Rd,EH11.............. (0131) 337 7936
Granton Baptist Church,29 Crewe Rd Gardens,EH5..... (0131) 552 0915
Granton Parish Church,Boswall Parkway,EH5.............. (0131) 552 3033
Greenbank Parish Church,Braidburn Terrace,EH10...... (0131) 447 9969
Greenside Parish Church,Royal Terrace,EH7.............. (0131) 556 5588
Greyfriars Tolbooth & Highland Kirk,
1 Greyfriars Place,EH1.............. (0131) 225 1900
Holy Cross Catholic Church,11 Bangholm Loan,EH5.... (0131) 552 3957
Holy Name Catholic Church,
Shrub Cottage Station Rd,Oakley.............. **New Oakley (01383)** 850335
Holy Trinity Church,
Hailesland Place,Wester Hailes,EH14.............. (0131) 442 3304
Holy Trinity Metropolitian Community Church,
PO Box 12433,Edinburgh,EH11.............. (0131) 347 8699
Inveresk Church Hall,
21a Dalrymple Loan,Musselburgh,EH21.............. (0131) 665 0713
Kilconquhar Parish Church,Main St.............. **Elie (01333)** 330685
Kilrenny Parish Church,Kilrenny........... **Anstruther (01333)** 310810
Kingdom Hall of Jehovah's Witnesses,
Tweed Brae.............. **Peebles (01721)** 729661

Kings Church Kelso,45-47 Roxburgh St........... **Kelso (01573)** 225177
Kirkcaldy Spiritualist Centre,
13 Kirk Wynd.............. **Kirkcaldy (01592)** 643645
Leith Baptist Church,27-29 Madeira St,EH6.............. (0131) 553 4488
Leslie Baptist Church,
82 Barnton Place.............. **Glenrothes (01592)** 754662
48 North St,Leslie.............. **Glenrothes (01592)** 745106
Leven Parish Church,Durie St.............. **Leven (01333)** 423969
Liberton Kirk,5a Kirkgate,EH16.............. (0131) 664 3067
Liberty Church,
PO Box 14559,Dunfermline,KY11 4WG... **Dunfermline (01383)** 733970
Limekilns Parish Church,Church St.......... **Limekilns (01383)** 873337
Link Christian Fellowship,
39 Priory Lane.............. **Dunfermline (01383)** 739169
Linktown Church,Nicol St.............. **Kirkcaldy (01592)** 641080
Livingston Baptist Church,
Cedarbank,Livingston,EH54.............. 01506 49
Livingston Mosque & Community Centre,
1 Craigshill Rd.............. **Livingston (01506)** 43
Lochgelly Baptist Church,Station Rd........ **Lochgelly (01592)** 78
Lochgelly Macainsh Church Of Scotland,
82 Main St.............. **Lochgelly (01592)** 78
London Road Church of Scotland,1a Easter Rd,EH7.... (0131) 661
Longniddry Parish Church,Elcho Rd......**Longniddry (01875)** 85
Marchmont St. Giles Parish Church,
1a Kilgraston Rd,EH9.............. (0131) 447
Mayfield Salisbury Church,Mayfield Rd,EH9.............. (0131) 667
(0131) 667
Melrose Parish Church,
Weirhill St. Marys Rd.............. **Melrose (01896)** 82
Methodist Church in Scotland,
Central Hall,2 West Tollcross,EH3.............. (0131) 221
Queensferry Rd,Rosyth.............. **Inverkeithing (01383)** 41
1 Junction Place,Leith,EH6.............. (0131) 555
Methodist Church & Centre Nicolson Square,EH8.............. (0131) 662
Morningside Baptist Church,Morningside Rd,EH10..... (0131) 447
Morningside Braid,Nile Gro,EH10.............. (0131) 447
Morningside United Church,
15 Chamberlain Rd,EH10.............. (0131) 447
Muirhouse St. Andrews Church,
42 Pennywell Gardens,EH4.............. (0131) 476
Murrayfield Parish Church,
Church Hall,2b Ormidale Terrace,EH12.............. (0131) 337
Musselburgh Congregational Church,
Link St,Musselburgh,EH21.............. (0131) 665
New Life Christian Fellowship,
12 Newbigging,Musselburgh,EH21.............. (0131) 665
New Restalrig Parish Church Hall,
1a Willowbrae Rd,EH8.............. (0131) 661
Newcraigs Evangelical Church,
Forres Drive.............. **Kirkcaldy (01592)** 20
Niddrie Mission,12 Hay Drive,EH16.............. (0131) 652
North Esk Church,Bridge St,Musselburgh,EH21.............. (0131) 665
North Leith Parish Church,1a Madeira Place,EH6........ (0131) 553
Oblates of Mary Immaculate,St. Mary Star of the Sea Church,
106 Constitution St,Leith,EH6.............. (0131) 554
Old St. Pauls Church,39 Jeffrey St,EH1.............. (0131) 556
Orthodox Church of St. Andrew,
1-2 Meadow Lane,EH8.............. (0131) 667
Our Lady of Loretto & St. Michael,
17 Newbigging,Musselburgh,EH21.............. (0131) 665
Our Lady of Lourdes,
Bathgate Rd,Blackburn.............. **Bathgate (01506)** 65
Our Lady of Lourdes,
67 Aberdour Rd.............. **Dunfermline (01383)** 72
Our Lady & St. Bride's,
74 Stenhouse St.............. **Cowdenbeath (01383)** 51
Our Lady & St. Margaret's R.C Church,
48 Bridgend.............. **Duns (01361)** 88
Our Lady's of Currie,Balerno & Ratho,
222 Lanark Rd West,Currie,EH14.............. (0131) 449
Our Lady Star Of The Sea R.C Church,
9 Law Rd.............. **N Berwick (01620)** 89
Oxgangs Christian Fellowship,
1c Oxgangs Avenue,EH13.............. (0131) 441
Pakistan Association Mosque & Community Centre,
43-45 Annandale St,EH7.............. (0131) 556
Palmerston Place Church,10 Palmerston Place,EH12... (0131) 220
Parish of Kelso North & Ednam The,
Bowmont St.............. **Kelso (01573)** 22
Pathhead Parish Church,Church St........... **Kirkcaldy (01592)** 20
Peebles Old Parish Church,
Session House High St.............. **Peebles (01721)** 72
Peebles St.Andrews Leckie Parish Church,
Eastgate.............. **Peebles (01721)** 72
Pilrig St. Paul's Church of Scotland,Pilrig St,EH6....... (0131) 553
Portobello Old Parish Church,Bellfield St,EH15.......... (0131) 669
Portobello Spiritualist Church,20a Bath St,EH15....... (0131) 669
Priestfield Church,2 Marchhall Place,EH16.............. (0131) 667
Reid Memorial Church,182 West Savile Terrace,EH9.... (0131) 662

Rhema Church Edinburgh,
1 Dean Bridge,Queensferry Rd,EH4.............. (0131) 343 3
Rhema Church Kirkcaldy,131 Links St...... **Kirkcaldy (01592)** 206
Richmond Craigmillar Church,
229 Niddrie Mains Rd,EH16.............. (0131) 661
Rock, Edinburgh Elim Pentecostal Church The,
37 South Clerk St,EH8.............. (0131) 668
Rosyth Baptist Church Manse,
52 Woodside Avenue,Rosyth.............. **Inverkeithing (01383)** 413
Sacred Heart Catholic Church,26 Lauriston St,EH3...... (0131) 229
(0131) 229
Sacred Heart & St. Anthony The,
2a Wotherspoon Crescent.............. **Armadale (01501)** 73
Sacred Heart The,56 John St.............. **Penicuik (01968)** 67
St. Albert the Great,25 George Square,EH8.............. (0131) 650
St. Andrew,149 Main St,Davidsons Mains,EH4.............. (0131) 336
St. Andrew Blackadder Church,High St...**N Berwick (01620)** 89
St. Andrews Church Of Scotland,
Grange Terrace.............. **Bo'Ness (01506)** 82
St. Andrews High Church,
70 Millhill,Musselburgh,EH21.............. (0131) 665 7

Andrews R.C Church,126 Victoria St... Livingston (01506) 432141
Andrew's & St. George's Parish Church,
orge St,EH2... (0131) 225 3847
Andrews Scottish Episcopal Church,
mont Place... Kelso (01573) 224163
Anne's Church,Kaimes Rd,Corstorphine,EH12... (0131) 316 4740
Baldred's Episcopal Church,
May Terrace... N Berwick (01620) 892154
Bernard's Ballingry,
e Presbytery Main Rd,Glencraig... Ballingry (01592) 860225
Bryce Kirk,St. Brycedale Avenue... Kirkcaldy (01592) 640016
Catherine of Alexandria R C Church,
Captains Row,EH16... (0131) 664 1596
Catherines Argyle Church,61-63 Grange Rd,EH9... (0131) 667 7220
Columba,9 Upper Gray St,EH9... (0131) 667 1605
Columba's by The Castle Episcopal Church,
Johnston Terrace,EH1... (0131) 622 2277
Columba's Church,
dney St,Craigshill... Livingston (01506) 431482
Cuthbert's Catholic Church,
4 Slateford Rd,Edinburgh,EH14... (0131) 443 1317
Cuthbert's Parish Church,5 Lothian Rd,EH1... (0131) 229 1142
Davids Broomhouse Church,
oomhouse Crescent,EH11... (0131) 443 9851
Davids Church,George St... Bathgate (01506) 652641
Davids R C Church,41 Eskbank Rd,Dalkeith,EH22... (0131) 663 4286
George's West Church,58 Shandwick Place,EH2... (0131) 220 6301
(0131) 225 7001
Giles' Cathedral,High St,EH1... (0131) 225 4363
James Church Golden Acre,
b Inverleith Row,EH3... (0131) 624 7777
James's Catholic Church,
High St,Innerleithen... Peebles (01721) 720865
Josephs Catholic Church,
Rosetta Rd... Peebles (01721) 720865
John's Church of Scotland,
Johns Manse Hawthorn Rd... Galashiels (01896) 752573
John's Church Of Scotland,
eldrum Rd... Kirkcaldy (01592) 201723
Johns Evangelical Church,
ion Rd,Linlithgow,EH49... 01506 517031
John's R.C Church,
37 Admiralty Rd,Rosyth... Inverkeithing (01383) 412084
John the Baptist RC Church,
St. Ninians Rd,EH12... (0131) 334 1693
John the Evangelist,Princes St,EH2... (0131) 229 7565
John The Evangelist R.C Church,
Sandford Gardens,EH15... (0131) 669 5447
John Vianney,40 Fernieside Gardens,EH17... (0131) 658 1793
Joseph's Catholic Church,
wdenbeath Rd... Burntisland (01592) 872207
Joseph's Catholic Church,
eburn Crescent... Whitburn (01501) 740348
Joseph's Church,
a Broomhouse Place North,EH11... (0131) 443 3777
Josephs R.C Church,
0 Cocklaw St,Kelty... Inverkeithing (01383) 412084
Kenneth Church,Cupar Rd... Kennoway (01333) 351372
Kenneth's Lochore,
e Presbytery Main Rd,Glencraig... Ballingry (01592) 860225
Kentigern R C Church,
6-28 Parkgrove Avenue,EH4... (0131) 336 4984
Leonards Parish Church,
rucefield Avenue... Dunfermline (01383) 620106
Margaret,
ope View Loch Rd,South Queensferry,EH30... (0131) 331 1007
Margaret,149 Main St,Davidsons Mains,EH4... (0131) 336 1083
Margaret Mary R C Church,
Boswall Parkway,EH5... (0131) 552 4782
Margarets Parish Church,
28 Woodside Rd... Glenrothes (01592) 610310
Margaret's Parish Church,
76 Restalrig Rd South,EH7... (0131) 554 7400
(0131) 661 6225
Maries Church,101 Dunnikier Rd,KY2... 01592 592111
Marks Church,32 Durham Avenue,EH15... (0131) 669 9903
Mark's R.C Church,Oxgangs Avenue,EH13... (0131) 441 3915
Martins Church Hall,232 Dalry Rd,EH11... (0131) 337 9714
Martin's of Tours R C Church,High St... Tranent (01875) 610232
Mary Magdalene,16 Milton Crescent,EH15... (0131) 669 3611
Mary of The Assumption Catholic Church,
inlithgow Rd... Bo'Ness (01506) 822339
Mary's Cathedral,23 Palmerston Place,EH12... (0131) 225 6293
Mary's Catholic Church,Poldrate... Haddington (01620) 822138
Mary's Catholic Church,
Marys Bowmont St... Kelso (01573) 224725
Marys Metropolitan R.C Cathedral,
roughton St,EH1... (0131) 556 1798
Marys R C,48 Main St,Pathhead... Ford (01875) 320266
Mary's & St. Columba's Catholic Church,
Livery St... Bathgate (01506) 655766
Mary's Scottish Episcopal Church,
almahoy,EH27... (0131) 333 1683
Mary, Star of the Sea Church,
06 Constitution St,Leith,EH6... (0131) 467 7449
Matthews,36 Carnethie St,Rosewell,EH24... (0131) 440 2150
Michael R.C Church,
3 Blackness Rd... Linlithgow (01506) 842145
Michael's Parish Church Office,
ross House... Linlithgow (01506) 842188
Ninian's Catholic Church,232 Marionville Rd,EH7... (0131) 661 2867
Ninians Church,High St... Galashiels (01896) 752967
Ninian's Church of Scotland,
44 St. Johns Rd,EH12... (0131) 334 7301
(0131) 539 6204
Ninian's Craigmalen Church Hall,
ongcroft Hall Philip Avenue... Linlithgow (01506) 670372
Ninians Episcopal Church,
9 Comley Bank Rd,EH4... (0131) 315 3163
Ninians Parish Church,
Ninians Church Hall Cawdor Drive... Glenrothes (01592) 610560
Patrick's Lochgelly,
he Presbytery Main Rd,Glencraig... Ballingry (01592) 860225
Patrick's R.C Church,
outh Grays Close,40 High St,EH1... (0131) 556 1973
Paul's Presbytery,Warout Rd... Glenrothes (01592) 752543
Pauls & St Georges Church,York Place,EH1... (0131) 556 1335
Peter-In-Chains,28 Hope St... Inverkeithing (01383) 413195
Peters Catholic Church,Forman Rd... Leven (01333) 425627
Peters Catholic Church,St. Peters Church House
armondean Centre... Livingston (01506) 438787
Peters Episcopal Church,
arsonage Rd... Galashiels (01896) 753118
Peters Episcopal Church,
ownsend Place... Kirkcaldy (01592) 206099
Peters Episcopal Church,
2 Windsor Gardens,Musselburgh,EH21... (0131) 665 2925
Peters R.C Church,77 Falcon Avenue,EH10... (0131) 447 2502

St. Peters Scottish Episcopal Church,
The Rectory, 45 Edderston Rd... Peebles (01721) 720571
St. Philip's,83 Kenilworth Rise... Livingston (01506) 414453
St. Pius X,St. Pius Presbytery Brodick Rd... Kirkcaldy (01592) 261901
St. Stephen's Centre The,
Stockbridge Parish Church St. Stephen St,EH3... (0131) 556 2661
(0131) 557 5846
St. Stephen's Comely Bank Church,
10 Comely Bank Rd,EH4... (0131) 315 4616
St. Theresa's Catholic Church,
41 Main St,East Calder... Mid Calder (01506) 880918
St. Thomas' Junction Road Parish Church,
123 Great Junction St,EH6... (0131) 555 6332
St. Thomas's Scottish Episcopal Church,
75-79 Glasgow Rd,EH12... (0131) 316 4292
Salvation Army The,
Corbie Rd... Bo'Ness (01506) 828502
Cowdenbeath Corps Stenhouse St... Cowdenbeath (01383) 512752
Pilmuir St... Dunfermline (01383) 723161
17 Victoria Park,Fauldhouse,Bathgate... Fauldhouse (01501) 770351
Caskieberran Rd... Glenrothes (01592) 757909
Croft Rd... Hawick (01450) 375075
Cairns St East... Kirkcaldy (01592) 640474
125 High St... Kirkcaldy (01592) 265928
Kingsport Avenue... Livingston (01506) 431339
6 Nelson Avenue... Livingston (01506) 433754
Auchterderran Rd... Lochgelly (01592) 783410
1 East Adam St,EH8... (0131) 667 4313
23 Kirk St,EH32... 01875 815125
Kirk St,Prestonpans,EH32... 01875 813089
Portobello Corps,48 Bath St,EH15... (0131) 669 7706
Sancta Maria Abbey,Nunraw,Haddington... Garvald (01620) 830223
Garvald (01620) 830228
Saughtonhall United Reformed Church,
87 Saughtonhall Drive,EH12... (0131) 337 8733
Scottish Episcopal Church,
St. Anne's Church,1 Westgate... Dunbar (01368) 865711
Good Shepherd,9 Upper Coltbridge Terrace,EH12... (0131) 337 2698
St. Peters Lutton Place,EH8... (0131) 667 9838
Selkirk Parish Church (With Ashkirk),
High St... Selkirk (01750) 20078
Seventh Day Adventist Church,
61 Boswall Parkway,Edinburgh... Dunfermline (01383) 731315
South Leith Baptist Church,Casselbank St,EH6... (0131) 553 2344
South Leith Parish Church,6 Henderson St,EH6... (0131) 554 2578
Southview Evangelical Church,Crosshill... Chirnside (01890) 818217
Stenhouse St. Aidan's Church,Chesser Avenue,EH14... (0131) 443 9452
Stockbridge Parish Church,7b Saxe Coburg St,EH3... (0131) 332 0122
Strathbrock Parish Church,
Church Hall Thomson Court,Uphall... Broxburn (01506) 856433
Subud Edinburgh Centre,
Bankhead Farm,South Queensferry,EH30... (0131) 331 1647
Templehall Parish Church,Beauly Place... Kirkcaldy (01592) 202514
The Christian Community,21 Napier Rd,EH10... (0131) 229 4514

THE ROCK

ELIM PENTECOSTAL CHURCH
"A Contemporary Church With A Permanent Message"
For More Information Contact
37 South Clerk St, Edinburgh EH8
T: 0131 668 3516 E: office@rockelim.com
Or Visit Our Site www.rockelim.com

Tranent Christian Centre,
3a Winton Place... Tranent (01875) 614500
True Jesus Church,
15a East Fettes Avenue,EH4... (0131) 343 2459
(0131) 343 1397
7 Gifford Park,EH8... (0131) 667 8176
Viewfield Baptist Church,
2 Viewfield Terrace... Dunfermline (01383) 620465
Viewforth Church,104 Gilmore Place,EH3... (0131) 229 7659

VIEWFORTH CHURCH HALLS

Halls And Rooms Available For Rent
Rooms Available For 6-150 People
Suitable For All Occasions
Tel: 0131 229 1917
www.viewforth.org
email: admin@viewforth.org
104 Gilmore Place, Edinburgh

Viewforth Parish Church,Viewforth St... Kirkcaldy (01592) 651238
Vine Church The,131 Garvock Hill... Dunfermline (01383) 736320
Wardie Parish Church,Primrose Bank Rd,EH5... (0131) 551 3847
Wemyss Parish Church,
33 Main Rd,East Wemyss... Buckhaven (01592) 713260
Wester Hailes Baptist Church,
Clovenstone Park,EH14... (0131) 453 4206
Whitburn Christian Fellowship,
266 West Main St... Whitburn (01501) 743481
Whitburn Pentecostal Church,
Reveston Lane... Whitburn (01501) 741447
World Conquerors Christian Centre,9 Lorne St,EH6... (0131) 555 2966

PLANBOARD EQPT

See: Office eqpt retailers

PLANNING CONSULTANTS

See also: Architects
Engineers - consulting
Flood Protection
Property development

A.M.G Plans,23 Glenlee Avenue,EH8... (0131) 661 1939
Allen Vance Associates,
3 Merchiston Bank Avenue,EH10... (0131) 452 9845
Barton Willmore Partnership,12 Alva St,EH2... (0131) 220 6002
Buchanan Colin & Partners,4 Saint Clome St,EH3... (0131) 226 4693
Campbell Colin Associates,55 East Trinity Rd,EH5... (0131) 552 4161
Campbell Kit Associates,
Chuckie Pend,24a Morrison St,EH3... (0131) 229 1006
Derek Scott
21 Lansdowne Crescent, Edinburgh EH12 5EH... 0131 535 1103
www.derekscottplanning.com
DKA Town Planning Consultants,
11 Wemyssfield... Kirkcaldy (01592) 268515
Drew Mackie Associates,10 Winton Grove,EH10... (0131) 445 5930
Farningham Mccreadie Partnership,
65 York Place,EH1... (0131) 525 8400
Hargest & Wallace Planning Ltd,
3 Clarendon Crescent,EH4... (0131) 332 2888

JENKINS & MARR ARCHITECTS & PLANNING CONSULTANTS
Email: info@jenkinsmarr.co.uk
Website: www.jenkinsmarr.co.uk
Abercromby Chambers,13 Abercromby Place,Edinburgh,
EH3 6LB... Tel 0131 558 8811
Fax 0131 558 8822

Kirk David & Associates,9 Commercial Rd... Leven (01333) 425699
Lowland Planning Associates,
Woodmuir Kirk Woodmuir Rd,Breich... Fauldhouse (01501) 772717
Mears Sir Frank Associates,24 Minto St,EH9... (0131) 662 9922
Orlowski David,6 Greenhill Gardens,EH10... (0131) 452 9300
PPCA Town Planners & Landscape Architects,
25 Alva St,EH2... (0131) 225 1225
Robinson Associates,Quadrant,17 Bernard St,EH6... (0131) 555 5150
Royal Fine Art Commission for Scotland,
Bakehouse Close,146 Canongate,EH8... (0131) 556 6699

The Royal Town Planning Institute

Each of these practices is registered with the RTPI as offering the services of at least one Chartered Town Planner or legal member of the RTPI who operates to the Institute's Code of Professional Conduct

AMG PLANNING AND DESIGN
Alexander Gordon
23 Glenlee Avenue
Edinburgh **Tel 0131-661 1939**
EH8 7HQ **Fax 0131-661 1939**
Email: alex.gordon@btclick.com
Website: www.amgplanning.co.uk

DKA PLANNING
11 Wemyssfield
Kirkcaldy
KY1 1XN **Tel/Fax (01592) 268515**
Email: alan.pollock@tiscali.co.uk

HALLIDAY FRASER MUNRO
Stanhope House
Stanhope Place
Edinburgh **Tel 0131-347 9920**
EH12 5HH **Fax 0131-347 9930**

For further information on Chartered Town Planners consult www.rtpiconsultants.co.uk

RPS CONSULTANTS LTD
45 Timberbush Bernard St Leith Edinburgh... 0131 555 5011
Smart Robert G,18 Campbell Avenue,EH12... (0131) 337 1581

TPS TOWN PLANNING SERVICES

Planning Applications & Appeals
Urban & Rural Regeneration
Project Co-ordination & Feasability Studies
Master Planning

Tel: 0131 272 2775
C B C House, 24 Canning St, Edinburgh, EH3 8EG

TPS Town Planning Services,
CBC House, 24 Canning St,EH3... (0131) 272 2775
Turley Associates,32 Alva St,EH2... (0131) 225 1717
Urban Design Solutions,179 Gilmore Place,EH3... (0131) 229 1241
Walker Suzanne,
46 Tantallon Gardens,Bellsquarry... Livingston (01506) 418195

PLANNING SUPERVISORS

See also: Architects
Architectural services
Engineers - consulting
Health & safety consultants
Quantity surveyors
Surveyors - building

Adamson, David & Partners,
32 Rutland Square, Edinburgh, EH1 2BW... Tel: 0131 229 7351
Fax: 0131 228 4523

Adamson, David & Partners,
Elizabeth House,Carberry Road,Kirkcaldy,
KY1 3PA... Tel: 01592 641116
Fax: 01592 641119

CLASSIFICATION CONTINUED ➤

Reference /

List of Works

22_____Lecture

1996
Installation with 30 chairs,
slide projector, amp, speakers,
screen, 39 slides
Dimensions variable
Commissioned by Galleri
Index, Stockholm, as part of
Sawn Off
Photo p.23: Tord Lund

26_____Urban Sanctuary

Edinburgh / 1997
Public artwork in the form
of a publication
Designed by Hector Pottie
and Tayburn Ltd
Published by Armpit Press,
Glasgow, ISBN 0-9523565-7-0
Edition of 1,000
Commissioned by
Stills Gallery, Edinburgh
Project managed by
Independent Public Arts Ltd,
Edinburgh
Photo p.27: Alan Dimmick

36_____Villa Savoye

1997
Installation with 30 chairs,
slide projector, amp, speakers,
screen, 80 slides
Dimensions variable
First shown in *Correspondences*,
Martin-Gropius Bau, Berlin, and
Scottish National Gallery of
Modern Art, Edinburgh

40_____Pigeon Lofts

1997
Installation with 30 chairs,
slide projector, amp, speakers,
screen, 39 slides
Dimensions variable
Commissioned by Kunsthalle Bern
Photo p.41: Roland Aellig

44_____Demolition in Progress

Berlin / 1997
Public artwork in the
Pavillon der Volksbühner, Berlin
Produced in collaboration with
Thomas Bechinger as part of
Blind Date, a series of
collaborations between curators
and artists initiated by Susanne
Gaensheimer and Maria Lind

46_____Minster

1998
Installation with 30 chairs,
slide projector, amp, speakers,
screen, 80 slides and printed
pamphlet
Dimensions variable
Commissioned by Tate Gallery
Liverpool as part of
Artranspennine98

50_____A Public Announcement

Stirling / 1998
8 two-colour text screenprints,
150 x 100cm; 8 colour
photographs, 51 x 76cm;
digital recording of male
voice reading the 8 texts,
running time 2 minutes
Public installation of one
screenprint per month
November 1998 – June 1999
Upper Craigs, Stirling
Commissioned by
The Changing Room, Stirling
Photo p.51: Alan Dimmick

54_____A Manifesto for Bournville

1999
Framed black and white
photograph, 110 x 240cm
Commissioned as part of
In the Midst of Things, Bournville,
1999; first installed in a disused
underpass in Bournville

56_____Landmark Portraits

1999 –
Ongoing series of colour
photographs, each 61 x 91cm

62_____Fourteen Churches of
Münster

2000
Single-screen video,
running time 14 minutes;
flight map 42 x 59cm
Commissioned by the
Westfälischer Kunstverein,
Münster, as part of *Inside Out*

66_____International Style

London / 2000
Two-screen video installation
with sound, running time
18 minutes
Commissioned by the
Architectural Association,
London

68_____The Lamp of Sacrifice,
161 Places of Worship,
Birmingham 2000

2000
Sculptural installation, cardboard
Dimensions variable
Commissioned by Ikon Gallery,
Birmingham as part of
as it is. Made in the
gallery by the artist during
the exhibition
Photo pp.69–71: Gary Kirkham

Biography

Born Glasgow / 1967

Education / 1985 – 89
B A (Hons), Fine Art,
Glasgow School of Art

Solo Exhibitions / Projects
2004 /
Nathan Coley, The Fruitmarket
Gallery, Edinburgh
Show Home, City Arts Centre,
Dublin
Show Home, Milton Keynes
Gallery, Milton Keynes

2003 /
Black Tent, Portsmouth Cathedral,
Portsmouth *
Show Home, North Shields,
Newcastle upon Tyne *

2002 /
Ruskin's Road, Leidsche Rijn,
the Netherlands (as part of *Super
Utrecht*)
The Black Maria, The Physics
Room, (as part of *Scape: Art and
Industry Urban Biennale*)
Christchurch, New Zealand

2001 /
Nathan Coley and Bas Jan Ader,
Vilma Gold, London
The Italian Tower, Kielder
Reservoir, Northumberland
The Land Marked, Centro Cultural
de Belém, Lisbon *

2000 /
International Style, Architectural
Association, London
Nathan Coley (with de Rijke
/ de Rooji), Galerie Rüdiger
Schöttle, Munich

1999 /
Der Standard, Museum in
Progress, Vienna

1998 /
A Public Announcement,
The Changing Room, Stirling *

1997 /
*Urban Sanctuary: a public
artwork*, Stills Gallery,
Edinburgh *
Demolition in Progress
(collaboration with Thomas
Bechinger), Pavillon der
Volksbühner, Berlin (as part of
Blind Date) *

1996 /
Nathan Coley, Galleri Index,
Stockholm *

1992 /
Pure Ideas in a Wicked World,
Crawford Arts Centre,
St Andrews *

Selected Group Exhibitions
2004 /
*On Reason and Emotion, Biennale
of Sydney 2004* *
Art School, Bloomberg Space,
London
Tales of the City, Arte Fiera,
Bologna, 2004

2003 /
Independence, South London
Gallery, London
*Days Like These: Tate Triennial of
Contemporary British Art*, Tate
Britain, London *

2002 /
Recent Acquisitions, City Art
Centre, Edinburgh
Fabrications, Cube (Centre for
Understanding the Built
Environment), Manchester *
The Gap Show, Museum am
Ostwall, Dortmund *
Happy Outsiders, Zacheta
Panstwowa Galeria Sztuki,
Warsaw *

2001 /
Audit, Casino Luxembourg,
Luxemburg *
Believe, Westfälischer Kunstverein,
Münster
Here and Now, DCA, Dundee *
Making History, Cannock Chase,
Staffordshire
Circles 3, ZKM, Karlsruhe *
Local Motion, Galerie Für
Zeitgenössische Kunst, Leipzig

2000 /
Jahresgaben 2000, Westfälischer
Kunstverein, Münster.
as it is, Ikon Gallery, Birmingham *
*Contemporary Scottish Artists
Books*, Printed Matter, New York
Tabley, Tabley House, Knutsford
*Salon d'Art Contemporain de
Montrouge*, touring to
ICA, Lisbon *
What If, Moderna Museet,
Stockholm *
Without Day, City Arts Centre,
Edinburgh *
Continuum 001, CCA,
Glasgow
Inside Out, Westfälischer
Kunstverein, Münster *

1999 /
Blue Suburban Skies,
Photographers' Gallery, London
In the Midst of Things, Bournville,
Birmingham *
School Reunion, Anthony
Wilkinson Gallery, London
Exhibition without an exhibition,
Leipzig
Threshold, Travelling Gallery,
Edinburgh

1998 /
In Visible Light, Moderna Museet,
Stockholm *
Strolling, Museum of Modern Art
at Heidi, Melbourne *
Artranspennine98, Tate Gallery
Liverpool *

Nettverk – Glasgow, Museum of Contemporary Art, Oslo*

1997 /
Correspondences, Martin-Gropius Bau, Berlin, Scottish National Gallery of Modern Art, Edinburgh *
Glasgow, Kunsthalle Bern, Bern *
A Scottish Collection, Berwick Gymnasium Gallery, Berwick
Blueprint, Glasgow Print Studio, Glasgow *
Wish you were here too, 83 Hill Street, Glasgow

1996 /
Girls' High, Old Fruitmarket, Glasgow *
Try, Royal College of Art, London

1995
Swarm, Travelling Gallery, Edinburgh *
Cameraless Photography, National Museum of Photography, Film and Television, Bradford

1994 /
New Art in Scotland, CCA, Glasgow, Aberdeen Art Gallery *
Riviera, Oriel Mostyn, Llandudno *
Go! – The Soccer Show, Mark Boote Gallery, New York

1993 /
Pure Fiction, Intermedia Gallery, Glasgow
Exposure, CCA, Glasgow
Five from Transmission, Artemisia Gallery, Chicago

1992 /
Love at First Sight, The Showroom, London
Lux Europae, Edinburgh

1991 /
Speed, Transmission Gallery, Glasgow
Windfall '91, Seamen's Mission, Glasgow *

1990 /
Fem fra Glasgow, Hordaland Kunstner Centrum, Bergen
Dependents, Transmission Gallery, Glasgow

* denotes catalogue

Awards
2003 /
Artist Award, Scottish Arts Council

2001 /
Henry Moore Fellowship, Duncan of Jordanstone College of Art, University of Dundee
Creative Scotland Award, Scottish Arts Council

2000 /
Scottish Cultural Enterprise, 'Scotland's Year of the Artist', Public Art Initiative Scheme, Scottish Arts Council

1997 /
RSA, Art for Architecture Award

1996 /
Artist Award, Scottish Arts Council

Residencies
2002 /
Lockerbie, The Scottish Court in the Netherlands, Holland (unofficial)

2000 /
Paisley University, Chemistry Department

1992 /
Crawford Arts Centre, St Andrews

Bibliography

Solo
Catalogues / Publications
2003 /
Black Tent, Art and Sacred Places,
London

2000 /
Fourteen Churches of Münster,
Westfälischer Kunstverein,
Münster

1998 /
A Public Announcement,
The Changing Room, Stirling

1997 /
Urban Sanctuary, Stills
Gallery, Edinburgh

1992 /
Pure Ideas in a Wicked World
Crawford Arts Centre, St Andrews

Group
Catalogues / Publications
2004 /
Tales of the City, Arte Fiera,
Bologna, 2004

2003 /
Days Like These, Tate Britain,
London

2002 /
*Scape: Art and Industry Urban
Arts Biennale Annual*,
Art and Industry Biennale Trust,
Christchurch
Fabrications, Cube Gallery,
Manchester
Happy Outsiders, Zachata
Panstwowa Galeria Sztuki,
Warsaw
The Gap Show, Museum am
Ostwall, Dortmund

2001 /
Circles, ZKM, Karlsruhe
From Work to Text, Centro
Cultural de Belém, Lisbon

Audit, Casino Luxembourg
Here and Now, DCA, Dundee
In the Midst of Things,
Bournville, Staffordshire

2000 /
as it is, Ikon Gallery, Birmingham
What If, Moderna Museet,
Stockholm
*Breathing Cities: Visualising
Urban Movement*, August /
Birkhäuser, London
Without Day, Pocketbooks,
Edinburgh

1999 /
*Exhibition without an
exhibition*, Leipzig
Threshold, Travelling Gallery,
Edinburgh

1998 /
Demolition in Progress,
Blind Date, Munich
Invisible Light, Moderna
Museet, Stockholm
Strolling, Museum of Modern
Art at Heidi, Melbourne
Artranspennine98, August Media,
London
Neetwerk Glasgow, Museum for
Samtidskunst, Oslo

1997 /
Correspondences,
Scottish National Gallery of
Modern Art, Edinburgh
Glasgow, Kunsthalle Bern,
Bern
Blueprint, Glasgow Print Studio

1996 /
Girls' High, Old Fruitmarket,
Glasgow
Try, Royal College of Art,
London

1995 /
Swarm, Travelling Gallery,
Edinburgh

1993 /
New Art in Scotland, CCA,
Glasgow
Riviera, Oriel Mostyn, Llandudno
Lux Europae, Edinburgh

1991 /
Windfall '91, Seamen's Mission,
Glasgow

Selected articles /
2004 /
Tim Cornwell, 'An act of blind faith'
The Scotsman, 20 March
Tim Cornwell, 'Lockerbie trial's
witness box to be part of museum'
The Scotsman, 17 February

2003 /
Annie Fletcher, 'Kamp Zeist',
Metropolis M, June / July
Jay Merrick, 'When we were
prefab', *The Independent Review*,
10 June
Paul Usherwood, 'Nathan
Coley – Show Home', *Art Monthly*,
August
Richard Dorment, 'Serious
pleasure', *The Daily Telegraph*,
26 February
Jes Fernie, 'Architectural
Dialogues', *a-n MAGAZINE*,
January

2002 /
Alison Green, 'Nathan Coley and
Bas Jan Ader', *Zingmagazine*,
Issue 17, Autumn
Joana Gorjao Henriques, 'Artista,
arqueologo, provocador de
historias', *Publico*, 21 February

2001 /
Nigel Prince, 'Nathan Coley – AA',
Untitled, Spring
Giles Sutherland, 'Kamp Zeist ',
Sculpture Matters, Issue 13,
Scottish Sculpture Trust,
Spring

2001 /
Lynn MacRitchie, 'Private lives
on public view', *Financial
Times*, 8 August

1997 /
Sarah Urquhart, 'Now for a
real eye opener', *The Herald*,
11 December
Mark Irving, 'Searching for
Sanctuary', *Blueprint*,
November

Acknowledgements

Published by
The Fruitmarket Gallery
45 Market Street
Edinburgh EH1 1DF
Tel: +44 (0) 131 225 2383
Fax: +44 (0) 131 220 3130
info@fruitmarket.co.uk
www.fruitmarket.co.uk

Jon Bewley & Jonty Tarbuck
Locus+ Publishing Ltd
Room 17, 3rd Floor
Wards Building
31 – 39 High Bridge
Newcastle upon Tyne
Tel: +44 (0) 191 233 1450
Fax: +44 (0) 191 233 1451
locusplus@newart.demon.co.uk
www.locusplus.org.uk

Distributed by
Art Data, London
Tel: +44 (0) 20 8747 1061

Produced by
The Fruitmarket Gallery,
Edinburgh

Edited by Fiona Bradley

Designed by Elizabeth McLean

Printed in an edition of 1,500
by Specialblue, London
Printed in the UK

ISBN 1 899377 21 2

The Fruitmarket Gallery
is supported by the
Scottish Arts Council
Scottish Charity No.
SC 005576

Locus+ is supported by
Arts Council England, North East

We thank the writers and
photographers who gave
permission to reproduce the texts
and illustrations in this book

Cover: Nathan Coley, *The Lamp
of Sacrifice, 161 Places of
Worship, Birmingham 2000*

Our thanks to
Sophie Allen, Nick Barley,
Geraldine Barlow, Susanna
Beaumont, Thomas Bechinger,
Lewis Biggs, Jürgen Bock, Greg
Bond, Christine Borland, Kari J
Brandtzaeg, Katrina Brown, Jenny
Brownrigg, Hilde de Brujin, Mike
Campbell, Isabel Carlos, Chris
Coles, Lise Connellan, Mark
Cousins, Andrew Crichton, Erick
Davidson, Alan Dimmick, Claire
Doherty, Anna Douglas, Juliana
Engberg, Rosemary Forde,
Susanne Gaensheimer, John
Green, Graham Gussin, Keith
Hartley, Maria Hlavajova, Mary
Horlock, Henrike Ingenthron,
Rebecca King Lassman, Boris
Kremer, Chaja Lang, Maria Lind,
Ulrich Loock, Lyndsay Mann,
Francis McKee, Kate Montgomery,
Judith Nesbitt, Tony Nolan, Irini-
Mirena Papadimitriou and Lisa
Bosse, Hector Pottie, Nigel Prince,
Jemma Read, Dave Renton,
Alison Rodgers, Natalie Rudd,
Stuart Russell, Peter Sharpe,
Jackie Shearer, Ross Sinclair,
Lisette Smits, Sharon and Alex
Summers, Kate Tregaskis, Gavin
Wade, Clarrie Wallis, Paula
Wantman, Jonathan Watkins,
Angela Weight

Published to coincide with
Nathan Coley, The Fruitmarket
Gallery, Edinburgh
22 May – 19 July 2004

The exhibition included
*The Lamp of Sacrifice, 286
Places of Worship, Edinburgh
2004,* the first Bloomberg /
Fruitmarket Gallery New
Commission.
    Bloomberg is a global,
multimedia news and information
company which runs an
expanding programme of art
sponsorship and philanthropy in
support of emerging international
artists. Bloomberg is particularly
proud that their sponsorship
builds on a previous association
with Nathan Coley, who made part
of *The Lamp of Sacrifice, 286
Places of Worship, Edinburgh
2004* during his residency at
Bloomberg SPACE's *Art School*
exhibition in London
in February 2004.

Exhibition supported by
Henry Moore Foundation
and The Russell Trust

Scottish
Arts Council

ARTS COUNCIL
ENGLAND

Bloomberg